Judicial Statistics

England and Wales for the year 2005

Presented to Parliament
by the Secretary of State for Constitutional Affairs and Lord Chancellor
by Command of Her Majesty

May 2006

Cm 6799

£27.00

Previous Reports

2005	Cmnd.	6799
2004	Cmnd.	6565
2003	Cmnd.	6251
2002	Cmnd.	5863
2001	Cmnd.	5551
2000	Cmnd.	5223
1999	Cmnd.	4786
1998	Cmnd.	4371
1997	Cmnd.	3980
1996	Cmnd.	3716
1995	Cmnd.	3290
1994	Cmnd.	2891
1993	Cmnd.	2623
1992	Cmnd.	2268
1991	Cmnd.	1990
1990	Cmnd.	1573
1989	Cmnd.	1154
1988	Cmnd.	745
1987	Cmnd.	428
1986	Cmnd.	173
1985	Cmnd.	9864
1984	Cmnd.	9599
1983	Cmnd.	9370

Introduction

The Department for Constitutional Affairs incorporates most of the responsibilities of the former Lord Chancellor's Department.

Contents of this volume

The statistics of this volume relate to the criminal and civil business of those courts in England and Wales for whose administration the Lord Chancellor is responsible. They also cover the work of some associated offices including the Public Guardianship Office, the Judicial Committee of the Privy Council and certain tribunals. Statistics relating to Northern Ireland courts are available separately from the Northern Ireland Court Service.

Each of chapters 1-8 includes a brief description of the function, constitution and jurisdiction of the courts or tribunals concerned together with an explanation of some of the procedures involved. Chapters 9 and 10 deal with the judiciary and taxation of costs and publicly funded legal services, respectively. In addition, commentary highlighting the major features of the statistics and any notable trends is included. All data relates to the calendar years shown, unless otherwise indicated. Reference to related statistical publications, where appropriate, is included.

The court structure

The present arrangements for the organisation and administration of the superior courts date from 1 January 1972, when the Courts Act 1971 came into operation.

The Lord Chancellor is responsible for the administration of the Supreme Court, which consists of the Court of Appeal, the High Court, and the Crown Court, and of the county courts and Magistrates' Courts (see chart on page 3). Administrative responsibility is exercised through the HM Courts Service which was created on 1 April 2005. Court Service staff are headed by a Regional Director in each of the seven regions in England and Wales. These regions are the Midland with its headquarters in Birmingham, the North Eastern (Leeds), the North Western (Manchester), the South Eastern and London (London), the Wales and Cheshire (Cardiff) and the South Western (Bristol). The map on page 4 shows the area covered by each region.

The Crown Court mainly deals with the more serious criminal offences which are committed for trial by magistrates' courts. The judges of the Crown Court are High Court judges (who also sit in the High Court to take civil business), circuit judges (who also sit in the county courts to try the less important civil cases), and part-time recorders. Overall supervision of the judicial work on each region is the responsibility of two High Court judges nominated by the

Lord Chief Justice to act as Presiding Judges on the region, under the Senior Presiding Judge for England and Wales.

Below the level of the High Court there are around 220 county courts, each of which has jurisdiction within its own district. They are presided over by circuit judges and district judges.

Judges are specially nominated by the Lord Chancellor for family work. This is referred to in more detail in Chapter 5.

One of the main features of the system is the flexible way in which it enables the judges to be deployed. High Court judges, circuit judges, and recorders are all judges of the Crown Court. As well as dealing with civil cases in the county courts, circuit judges may also be invited by the Lord Chancellor to sit from time to time as judges of the High Court for civil business. Recorders sit primarily in the Crown Court, but they may also sit on civil business.

Magistrates' Courts

From April 1992 the Lord Chancellor assumed responsibility for the administration of magistrates' courts. Statistics relating to criminal proceedings in these courts are dealt with in Chapter 7. Statistics relating to the family proceedings courts and the appointment of justices of the peace are dealt with in chapters 5 and 9 respectively in this edition of *Judicial Statistics*.

Symbols and conventions used

The following symbols are used in the tables of this volume:

–	nil
..	not available or not appropriate

Estimated figures based on sample data are rounded and distinguished by italic type.

Enquiries regarding this publication or requests for unpublished data should be addressed to:

HM Courts Service
Performance Directorate
4th Floor, Steel House, 11 Toothill Street,
London SW1H 9LJ

Editors: Alan Sealy

Alternative copies of this publication in Braille or large print formats can be made available if required. Production time will depend upon demand.

An outline of the court structure in England and Wales

This diagram is, of necessity, much simplified and should not be taken as a comprehensive statement on the jurisdiction of any specific court.

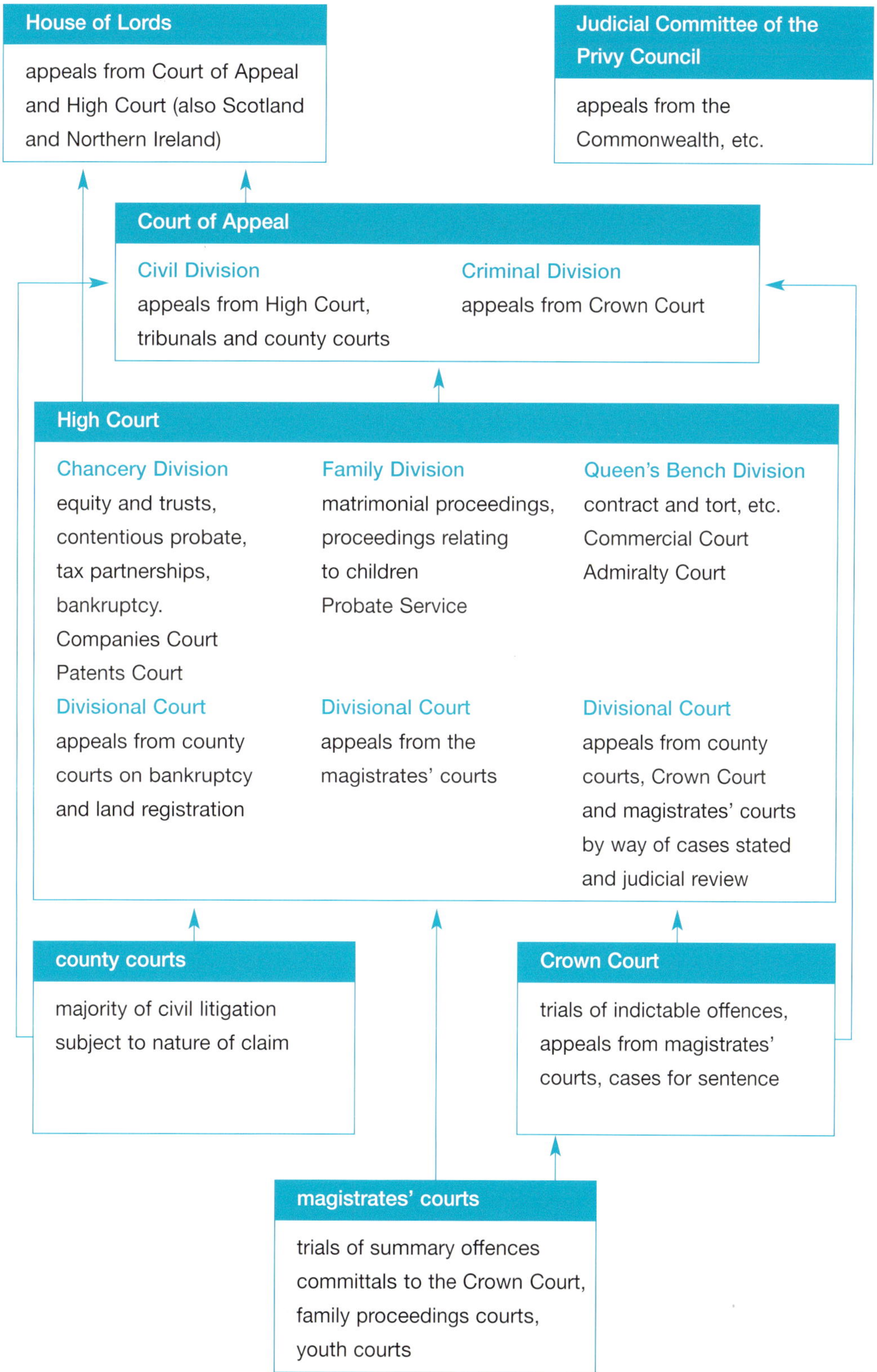

Region Boundaries of England and Wales

Appellate Courts

The various appellate courts are –

The Judicial Committee of the Privy Council – the final Court of Appeal for 24 Commonwealth territories and 6 independent Republics within the Commonwealth

The House of Lords – the Supreme Court of Appeal in Great Britain and Northern Ireland

The Court of Appeal – divided into the *Criminal Division* hearing appeals from the Crown Court and Courts Martial, and the *Civil Division* hearing appeals mainly against decisions in the High Court and county courts

The High Court – has three Divisions, Chancery Division (Chapter 2), Queen's Bench Division (Chapter 3) and Family Division (Chapter 5), each of which handles different types of civil work. It exercises an appellate jurisdiction through its three Divisions in such matters as bankruptcy, judicial review, 'case stated' (ruling whether a court or tribunal was wrong in law or in excess of its jurisdiction) and appeals from magistrates' courts in domestic matters including orders involving children

During 2005 –

- 75 appeals were disposed of by the Judicial Committee of the Privy Council **(Table 1.1)**
- over 52% of appeals disposed of by the House of Lords were allowed **(Table 1.4)**
- of the appeals heard by the Court of Appeal Criminal Division, over 37% against conviction and over 71.2% against sentence were allowed **(Table 1.8)**
- in the Civil Division of the Court of Appeal 1,177 final appeals were disposed of, nearly 38% of which were allowed **(Table 1.9)**
- appeals and applications entered in the Queen's Bench Division decreased by 3.9% **(Table 1.17)**

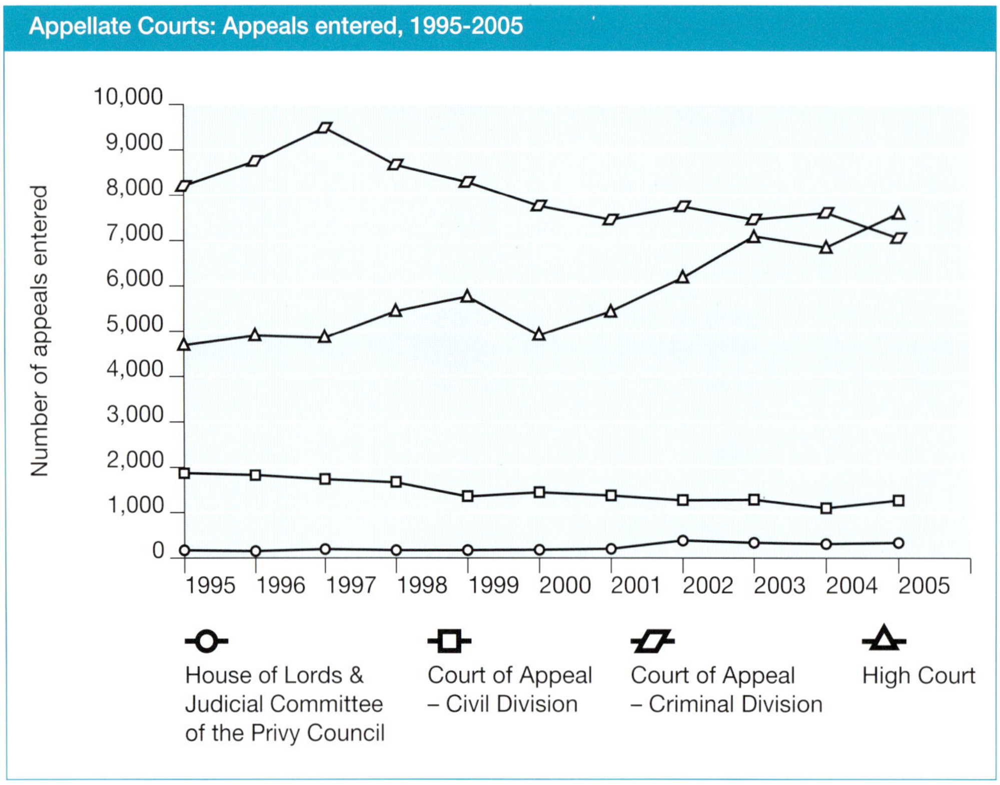

The Judicial Committee of the Privy Council

Introduction

The Judicial Committee of the Privy Council was given its name and established on its present statutory footing by the Judicial Committee Act 1833, but the origins of its overseas jurisdiction go back to medieval times when the Sovereign sought his Privy Council's advice on disputes arising in the Channel Islands, whence an appeal still lies. Today the Judicial Committee of the Privy Council has both a Commonwealth and a domestic jurisdiction.

In its Commonwealth jurisdiction, which is by far the largest part of its work, the Judicial Committee hears appeals from those independent Commonwealth countries which have retained the appeal to Her Majesty in Council or, in the case of Republics, to the Judicial Committee itself; it also hears appeals from the United Kingdom overseas territories. By agreement with the Sultan of Brunei, the Committee can hear appeals from the Brunei Court of Appeal, but in civil matters only, and gives its advice to the Sultan.

The Judicial Committee's domestic jurisdiction has four main elements:

a) appeals and references under the devolution statutes of 1998, which give the Judicial Committee jurisdiction to hear and determine "devolution issues", i.e. issues as to the functions and powers of the devolved legislative and executive authorities established in Scotland, Northern Ireland and Wales;

b) appeals from the Channel Islands and Isle of Man, which are analogous to Commonwealth appeals and are dealt with under the same rules;

c) appeals under the Veterinary Surgeons Act 1966 from decisions of the Disciplinary Committee of the Royal College of Veterinary Surgeons; until April 2003 appeals also lay from the professional conduct and other committees of the bodies governing the medical, dental and other health-care professions as well, but these now lie to the High Court;

(d) appeals against pastoral schemes under the Pastoral Measure 1983.

Leave to appeal to the Judicial Committee of the Privy Council is usually required. For Commonwealth civil appeals leave can in many cases be granted by the Court of Appeal of the country or territory concerned. For Commonwealth criminal appeals leave to appeal cannot be given by the Court of Appeal except where a question of constitutional interpretation arises. Leave to appeal is not required for devolution appeals from the Inner House of the Scottish Court of Session or appeals under the Veterinary Surgeons Act 1966. Where leave to appeal is required and cannot be given or has been refused by the Court of Appeal, the would-be appellant may apply by way of petition to the Judicial Committee for special leave to appeal. All such petitions in Commonwealth cases are dealt with at an oral hearing unless the respondent consents; but in devolution and Pastoral Measure cases they are dealt with on the papers unless they are referred for an oral hearing.

Commonwealth appeals and devolution appeals and references are normally heard by a board of five members of the Judicial Committee; other appeals and petitions are normally dealt with by a Board of three, which is the quorum.

More information about the Judicial Committee and its work, including the full text of recent judgments and statistics for 1996-2005, can be found on the Privy Council Office website, at www.pco.gov.uk.

The year's work

In 2005 the Judicial Committee sat on 106 days, a slight increase over the previous year. A total of 71 appeals were entered during the year and 41 petitions for special leave to appeal were dealt with. Trinidad and Tobago was the largest single source of appeals in 2005.

The Judicial Committee sat as a Board of nine to hear an appeal from the Attorney General of Jersey concerning provocation in relation to a person with the respondent's characteristics, a chronic alcoholic, who had killed his girlfriend while under the influence of alcohol.

In a petition from the Pitcairn Islands for directions on an appeal to be heard in 2006 the Board gave permission in principle for the proceedings to be filmed on a video camera, the method of transmission to Pitcairn to be agreed.

An appeal was heard from Jamaica regarding three bills designed to amend the Constitution and provide for the abolition of appeals to her Majesty in Council and make provision for appeals to Caribbean Court of Justice.

There were three appeals from Jamaica challenging the constitutionality of the mandatory death sentence.

Future prospects

Looking ahead, there may be an eventual decline in the Judicial Committee's volume of work. The last appeal under the Medical Act was disposed of in 2004. New Zealand, one of the largest single sources of appeals, legislated in 2003 to abolish appeals to the Privy Council for all appeals heard by the New Zealand Court of Appeal after the end of that year; at the end of 2005 there were three appeals from New Zealand still outstanding. Progress is being made on the establishment of the Caribbean Court of Justice, which will take over the Judicial Committee's appellate jurisdiction in respect of most of the Commonwealth countries in the Caribbean. Finally, under the Government's proposals for a new Supreme Court for the United Kingdom, the devolution jurisdiction of the Judicial Committee will be transferred to the Supreme Court, though the Judicial Committee and its jurisdiction will otherwise be unaffected.

Table 1.1
Judicial Committee of the Privy Council: Appeals entered and disposed of, showing results, 2005

		Appeals disposed of					
		Appeals disposed of after a hearing					
Courts from which appeals were brought	Number of appeals entered	Dismissed	Varied	Allowed	Without a hearing[1]	Total	Appeals pending at end of year
Overseas:							
Akrotiri and Dhekelia	–	–	–	1	–	1	–
Antigua and Barbuda	2	–	–	2	–	2	2
The Bahamas	11	–	1	1	1	3	16
Barbados	–	1	–	–	1	2	–
Belize	–	2	–	–	–	2	2
British Virgin Islands	3	–	–	–	1	1	3
Cayman Islands	4	1	–	–	–	1	4
Dominica	–	–	–	1	–	1	–
Gibraltar	–	–	–	1	–	1	–
Grenada	2	–	–	–	–	–	2
Guernsey	2	–	–	–	–	–	2
Isle of Man	2	–	–	1	–	1	2
Jamaica	15	5	–	3	–	8	16
Jersey	3	–	–	1	–	1	3
Mauritius	9	1	–	1	–	2	1
Montserrat	–	–	1	–	–	1	–
New Zealand	3	4	–	2	2	8	3
St. Christopher and Nevis	–	1	–	–	–	1	–
St Lucia	1	–	–	–	–	–	3
St Vincent and the Grenadines	1	–	–	–	–	–	1
Trinidad and Tobago	7	9	2	7	–	18	11
United Kingdom:							
Appeals under Veterinary Surgeons Act 1966	2	–	–	–	1	1	1
Appeals under the Scotland Act 1998	4	–	–	2	–	2	4
Total	**71**	**24**	**4**	**23**	**6**	**57**	**75**

[1] Dismissed for non-prosecution or withdrawn

Table 1.2
Judicial committee of the Privy Council: Petitions for special leave to appeal heard, granted and refused, 2004

	Granted	Refused	Total number heard
Country or jurisdiction of origin.			
The Bahamas	3	1	4
Belize	–	2	2
British Virgin Islands	2	–	2
Cayman Islands	–	2	2
Gibraltar	1	–	1
Grenada	–	2	2
Guernsey	1	1	2
Isle of Man	1	--	1
Jamaica	3	3	6
Jersey	-	1	1
Mauritius	3	1	4
New Zealand	2	–	2
Pitcairn Islands	–	1	1
St Vincent and the Grenadines	–	1	1
Trinidad and Tobago	2	5	7
Total	**18**	**20**	**38**

The House of Lords

The House of Lords is the final court of appeal in the United Kingdom of Great Britain and Northern Ireland. The judicial function of the House is exercised by twelve Lords of Appeal in Ordinary ("law lords"), together with other Lords of Appeal as required.

The House hears appeals on arguable points of law of general public importance which ought to be considered by the House at that time, bearing in mind that the causes will have already been the subject of judicial decision.

The judicial business of the House is administered by the Judicial Office, which is part of the House of Lords administration. Judgments of the House can be found on the Internet at *www.parliament.uk*. Further information about the role and work of the law lords can also be found on this site.

Civil appeals
An appeal lies to the House of Lords –

(a) from any order or judgment of the Court of Appeal in England, with the permission of that court or, if refused, by leave of the House of Lords, subject to restrictions in respect of specific matters

(b) from any order or judgment of any court in Scotland from which error or appeal lay on or immediately before 1 November 1876 by common law or by statute. Leave to appeal from an interlocutor of the Inner House of the Court of Session is not normally required

(c) from any order or judgment of the Court of Appeal in Northern Ireland, with the permission of that court or, if refused, by leave of the House of Lords, subject to statutory restrictions

(d) subject to statutory restrictions, direct from a decision of the High Court of Justice in England and Wales by leave of the House of Lords

(e) subject to statutory restrictions, direct from a decision of the High Court of Justice in Northern Ireland by leave of the House of Lords

Criminal appeals

An appeal lies, with leave, to the House of Lords at the instigation of the defendant or the prosecutor –

(a) from any decision of the Court of Appeal (Criminal Division) in England on an appeal to that court

(b) from any decision of the Courts-Martial Appeal Court on an appeal to that court

c) from any decision of the Court of Appeal in Northern Ireland on an appeal to that court

d) from any decision of the High Court of Justice in England and Wales in a criminal cause or matter

e) from any decision of the High Court of Justice in Northern Ireland in a criminal cause or matter

Leave may be granted by the court below or, if refused, by the House of Lords. Leave to appeal in a criminal cause or matter is only granted if it is certified by the court below that a point of law of general public importance is involved in the decision of that court, and if it appears to that court or to the House that the point is one that ought to be considered by the House. A certificate is not required for: an appeal from a decision of the High Court on a criminal application for habeas corpus; an appeal under s 5(4) of the Human Rights Act 1998; or in contempt of court cases where the decision of the court below was not a decision on appeal.

No appeal lies to the House of Lords from the High Court of Justiciary in Scotland.

Petitions for leave to appeal are referred to an Appeal Committee of three Lords of Appeal in Ordinary. Leave to appeal is usually determined on the basis of written submissions by the parties, but the Committee may decide to hear counsel before making a final decision on the application for leave.

During 2005, 240 petitions for leave to appeal were presented and 255 were disposed of, 79 of which were allowed.

Table 1.3

House of Lords: Petitions for leave to appeal presented and disposed of, showing results, 2005

		Petitions disposed of					
Courts from which appeals were brought	Number of petitions presented	Withdrawn	Allowed	Allowed on terms	Refused	Dismissed as inadmissable	Total
England and Wales:							
Court of Appeal							
Civil	186	2	61	–	113	24	200
Criminal	24	3	8	–	10	–	21
High Court							
Civil	6	–	2	–	2	3	7
Criminal	15	–	5	–	15	–	20
Scotland:							
Court of Session	–	–	–	–	–	–	–
Northern Ireland:							
Court of Appeal							
Civil	7	–	3	–	2	–	5
Criminal	1	–	–	–	–	1	1
High Court							
Civil	1	–	–	–	1	–	1
Criminal	–	–	–	–	–	–	–
Other:							
Courts Martial Appeal Court	–	–	–	–	–	–	–
Attorney General's reference	–	–	–	–	–	–	–
Total	**240**	**5**	**79**	**–**	**143**	**28**	**255**

Appeals are usually heard by Appellate Committees consisting of five Lords of Appeal sitting in a committee room of the House; but occasionally appeals are heard in the House itself. Hearings typically last two days. After the hearing, each member of the Committee writes his or her opinion; and the Committee reports these to the House at a sitting for judicial business, with counsel attending at the bar.

During 2005, 102 appeals were presented of which 75 were from the Civil Division of the Court of Appeal. A total of 87 appeals received judgment.

Table 1.4
House of Lords: Appeals presented and disposed of, showing the courts appealed from and results, 2005

		Appeals disposed of			
			Judgement		
Courts from which appeals were brought	Number of petitions presented	Without a judgment	Allowed	Dismissed	Total
England and Wales:					
Court of Appeal					
Civil	59	7	40	28	75
Criminal	5	–	8	4	12
High Court					
Civil	2	1	–	–	1
Criminal	7	2	–	5	7
Scotland:					
Court of Session	11	2	2	–	4
Northern Ireland:					
Court of Appeal					
Civil	3	1	1	–	2
Criminal	–	–	–	1	1
High Court					
Civil	–	–	–	–	–
Criminal	–	–	–	–	–
Other:					
Courts Martial Appeal Court	–	–	–	–	–
Attorney General's reference	–	–	–	–	–
Total	**87**	**11**	**53**	**38**	**102**

Table 1.5
House of Lords: civil appeals (England and Wales) presented from the Court of Appeal, disposed of by judgment in 2005 and categorised by subject matter

Subject matter	Total determined
Administrative	10
Commercial	2
Company	1
Contract	2
Crime	3
Discrimination	3
Employment	–
European Law	–
Family	4
Finance & Credit	–
Human Rights	19
Intellectual Property	1
International	3
Land	2
Planning	–
Practice & Procedure	2
Revenue	10
Sale of Goods	–
Tort	4
Trusts	2
Total	**68**

During 2004, 2 causes were referred to the Court of Justice of the European Communities for a ruling; one determination was received and 3 references were pending at the end of the year. The total number of days sat for judicial business was 120. (NB. More than one judicial Committee may sit at once. This means that on a single sitting day the House may hear more than one petition for leave to appeal, may hear two appeals concurrently, or may hear an appeal as well as petitions for leave to appeal). No peerage claim was heard this year and the Committee for Privileges Sub-Committee on Lords' Interests did not have to hear any allegation of non-compliance with the Code of Conduct for Members of the House of Lords.

Table 1.6
House of Lords: Judicial and Privileges days sat, 2005

Nature of Proceedings	
Sitting for judicial business	
Days Sat to hear petitions for leave	6
Days sat for a directions hearing	–
Days sat to hear appeals	114
Committee for Privileges	
Days sat to hear peerage claims	–
Days sat to hear Code of Conduct references	–

The Court of Appeal

The Court of Appeal is divided into two Divisions, criminal and civil. Its courtrooms and offices are situated in the Royal Courts of Justice in London. The judges of the Court of Appeal are the Lord Chief Justice, the Master of the Rolls and 37 Lords Justices. The President of the Family Division and the Vice-Chancellor of the Chancery Division also sit there for part of their time. The Criminal Division, presided over by the Lord Chief Justice and the Vice-President of the Criminal Division, hears appeals in criminal matters from the Crown Court. Courts are constituted from the Lord Chief Justice, Vice-President and Lords Justices assisted by High Court judges as required. The Civil Division, presided over by the Master of the Rolls, hears appeals mainly against decisions of the High Court and county courts and also of tribunals and certain other courts, such as the Patents Court. In the Civil Division, courts of two or three judges are normally constituted from the Master of the Rolls and the Lords Justices.

Criminal Division

During 2005, a total of 7,023 applications for leave to appeal were received, of which 1,661 were against conviction in the Crown Court and 5,178 against the sentence imposed. Of the applications for leave to appeal which were considered by a single judge, nearly 24.5% (360) of those seeking to appeal against conviction were granted as were just over 25.2% (1,541) against sentence (23% and nearly 32% respectively in 2004). Of those applications which were refused, 557 were renewed to the Full Court against conviction and 824 against sentence.

Table 1.7

Court of Appeal (Criminal Division): Results of applications for leave to appeal,1995-2004

	1995	1996	1997[1]	1998	1999	2000	2001	2002	2003[2]	2004	2005
Received:											
Conviction	2,393	2,288	2,318	2,099	2,104	2,068	1,943	1,914	1,787	1,782	1,661
Sentence	5,794	6,436	7,160	6,550	6,170	5,672	5,497	5,804	5,664	5,809	5,178
Other Receipts:	-	-	-	-	-	-	-	-	-	-	184
Total	**8,187**	**8,724**	**9,478**	**8,649**	**8,274**	**7,740**	**7,440**	**7,718**	**7,451**	**7,591**	**7,023**
Considered by single judge:											
Conviction:											
Granted	472	419	589	542	480	508	438	405	472	348	360
Refused	1,444	1,429	1,530	1,407	1,402	1,351	1,145	1,334	1,213	1,187	1,111
Sentence											
Granted	1,263	1,544	1,801	1,909	1,743	1,597	1,551	1,695	1,736	1,740	1,541
Refused	3,846	4,629	4,810	4,613	4,095	3,892	3,475	3,876	3,582	3,634	3,092
Total	**7,025**	**8,021**	**8,730**	**8,471**	**7,720**	**7,348**	**6,609**	**7,310**	**7,003**	**6,909**	**6,104**
Applications renewed:											
Conviction	579	474	665	668	637	551	422	457	561	545	557
Sentence	635	823	1,105	1,147	1,072	932	759	825	878	890	824
Total	**1,214**	**1,297**	**1,770**	**1,815**	**1,709**	**1,483**	**1,181**	**1,282**	**1,439**	**1,435**	**1,381**
Applications to renew granted by Full Court:											
Conviction	123	155	131	172	123	144	150	140	138	144	141
Sentence	151	146	391	377	306	291	240	252	338	283	326
Total	**274**	**301**	**522**	**549**	**429**	**435**	**390**	**392**	**476**	**427**	**467**

[1] From 1997, figures relate to applications rather than appellants

[2] Figures do not include applications made by Attorney General. In 2004, 5 applications by the Attorney General Under section 36 of the Criminal Justice Act 1972 were received, (compared to 3 in 2003) and 160 applications by Attorney General under section 36 of the Criminal Justice Act 1988 (unduly lenient sentences) were received (compared to 101 in 2003).

Of the appeals heard by the Full Court during 2005, over 37.1% (228) against conviction were allowed and over 71.2% (1,534) against sentence were allowed.

Table 1.8
Court of Appeal (Criminal Division): Results of appeal heard by Full Court, 1995-2005[1]

	1995	1996	1997	1998	1999	2000	2001	2002	2003	2004	2005
Conviction:											
Allowed	253	250	236	290	171	150	135	166	178	240	228
Dismissed	521	469	367	403	380	333	313	319	364	384	386
Sentence:											
Allowed	1,222	1,379	1,468	1,589	1,564	1,284	1,101	1,302	1,685	1,348	1,534
Dismissed	538	603	602	609	614	522	561	500	679	589	619
Number of retrials ordered	52	53	33	73	70	72	58	50	45	66	

[1] From 1997, figures relate to applications rather than appellants

Civil Division

Applications for permission to appeal remained stable at 2,430 over the last year, compared to 2,430 in 2004 and 3,448 in 2003. This reflects the fact that the universal requirement for permission to appeal is operating as a filter on the weight and quality of work coming before the court, as envisaged by CPR Part 52.

In the area of substantive appeals the Court has seen a continuing increase in appeals from Tribunals, issuing 253 in 2005 as opposed to 240 in 2004. Appeals from the Queens Bench Division have increased from 194 in 2004 to 349 in 2005. Appeals from the Chancery Division increased from 121 to 128.

Table 1.9

Court of Appeal (Civil Division): Final Appeals filed and disposed of, showing court appealed from and and results, 2005

		Disposed of					
	Filed	Allowed	Dismissed	Dismissed by consent	Struck out for failure to provide documents	Otherwise disposed of	Total
Court or tribunal appealed from							
Chancery	114	46	86	25	1	3	161
Revenue	12	6	4	–	–	–	10
Bankruptcy	23	5	8	3	–	2	18
Family Division	2		3	1	–	–	4
Queen's Bench	134	33	67	26	–	2	128
Queen's Bench Administrative Court	108	37	61	11	–	7	116
Queen's Bench Commercial	67	20	41	13	–	1	75
Queen's Bench Admiralty	3		4	2	–	–	6
County Court	277	98	144	41	1	3	287
County Court Family	17	11	8	1	–	–	20
County Court Admiralty	–	–	–	–	–	–	0
Lands Tribunal	3	–	2	–	–	1	3
Employment Appeal Tribunal	43	27	32	11	1	–	71
Asylum & Immigration Tribunal	110	22	3	3	–	–	28
Immigration Appeal Tribunal	140	124	57	20	–	1	202
Patents Court	26	5	16	4	–	–	25
Social Security Commissioner	16	7	8	2	–	1	18
Other Tribunals	8	1	3	1	–	–	5
Total	**1,103**	**442**	**547**	**164**	**3**	**21**	**1,177**

Table 1.10
Court of Appeal (Civil Division): Interlocutory Appeals filed and disposed of, showing the courts appealed from and results, 2005

	Filed	Disposed of: Allowed	Dismissed	Dismissed by consent	Struck out for failure to provide documents	Otherwise disposed of	Total
Chancery	3	2	7	2	–	1	12
Revenue	–	–	–	–	–	–	0
Bankruptcy	1	1	1	–	–	–	2
Family Division	25	9	15	2	–	–	26
Queen's Bench	25	8	18	10	1	–	37
Queen's Bench Administrative Court	3	1	–	–	–	1	2
Queen's Bench Commercial	7	2	7	1	–	–	10
Queen's Bench Admiralty	–	–	–	–	–	–	0
County Court	5	5	3	1	–	–	9
County Court Family	60	37	25	4	–	–	66
County Court Admiralty	–	–	–	–	–	–	0
Lands Tribunal	–	–	–	–	–	–	0
Employment Appeal Tribunal	2	–	–	–	–	–	0
Asylum & Immigration Tribunal	3	–	3	–	–	–	3
Immigration Appeal Tribunal	–	–	–	–	–	–	0
Patents Court	2	–	–	–	–	–	0
Social Security Commissioner	–	–	–	–	–	–	0
Other Tribunals	–	–	–	–	–	–	0
Total	**136**	**65**	**79**	**20**	**1**	**2**	**167**

Table 1.11
Court of Appeal (Civil Division): Applications set down and disposed of, 1995-2005

	Full Court[1]		Single Judge		Permission to Appeal		Registrar/ Master		Total	
Year	Filed	Disposed	Set down	Disposed	Set down	Disposed	Set down	Disposed	Set down	Disposed
1995	1,756	1,779	687	486	–	–	215	239	2,658	2,504
1996	655	593	80	67	1,930	1,790	240	210	2,905	2,660
1997	622	661	71	69	1,844	2,031	201	212	2,738	2,973
1998	715	715	165	144	1,897	1,934	68	128	2,845	2,921
1999	584	611	1,326	1,150	2,382	2,134	43	52	3,183	2,967
2000	437	566	304	262	2,411	2,604	68	62	3,210	3,494
2001	288	313	320	335	2,415	2,388	72	80	3,095	3,116
2002	314	329	274	267	2,434	2,391	70	74	3,092	3,061
2003	230	247	275	259	2,448	2,514	72	71	3,025	3,091
2004	225	251	260	261	2,430	2,402	97	92	3,159	3,116
2005	291	264	286	274	2,579	2,495	122	121	3,278	3,154

[1] Includes new 'leave to appeal' cases

The High Court

The three Divisions of the High Court exercise appellate jurisdiction in the following manner –

a) the Divisional Court of the Chancery Division hears appeals in revenue matters from the Commissioners of Taxes. All bankruptcy appeals from the county courts and from the High Court Registrars under the Insolvency Act 1986 are heard by a single judge of the Chancery Division

b) the Divisional Court of the Queen's Bench Division and the Administrative Court nominated judges, exercise jurisdiction in respect of –

  i) Judicial Review

  ii) appeals by way of 'case stated'

  iii) habeas corpus

  iv) committal for contempt committed in an inferior court or elsewhere (but not in connection with proceedings in the High Court)

  v) appeals and applications under various statutory provisions including those on planning matters under the Town and Country Planning Acts

c) the Divisional Court of the Family Division hears appeals from magistrates' courts in a wide variety of domestic matters including orders involving children. The appeals are entered at the Principal Registry in London

In the Administrative Court, supervisory jurisdiction, by way of judicial review, is exercised over the Crown Court (for matters not relating to trial on indictment), inferior courts and tribunals, and the actions and decisions of public bodies or Government ministers or other persons charged with the performance of public acts and duties. The remedy of judicial review is concerned with the legality and propriety of the decision-making process as distinct from the merits of the decision in question. It is only appropriate when all other avenues of appeal have been exhausted. The Court exercises control when deemed appropriate by making what are known as 'prerogative orders'. These may for example command a person or body to perform a duty, prohibit an inferior court or tribunal from exceeding its jurisdiction or quash the decision under challenge.

Appeals by way of case stated arise when a person is dissatisfied on a point of law with a decision of the Crown Court (for matters not relating to trial indictment), a magistrates' court or other tribunal. The court or tribunal concerned is required to 'state a case' by preparing a statement for the opinion of the High Court giving the facts and the reason for the decision and setting out the question for the High Court.

An application for a writ of habeas corpus is usually made to the Divisional Court but if no court is sitting a single judge may hear the matter. This procedure provides for a person detained in custody (e.g. in prison, police cell or elsewhere) to challenge the legality of his detention. If the imprisonment is found to be unlawful the court will order release but otherwise the person concerned is returned to custody.

In 2003 a new jurisdiction was added by S101 of the Nationality Immigration and Asylum Act 2002 – a statutory review of decisions of the Immigration Appeal Tribunal as to whether or not to grant permission to appeal.

Chancery

The number of bankruptcy appeals from county courts (102) accounted for 50.7% of disposals in 2005 (69% in 2004). Of these, 6 were allowed, 15 withdrawn or struck out and the remaining 81 dismissed after hearing.

Table 1.12
High Court – Chancery Division: Appeals and special cases from inferior courts and tribunals set down and determined, showing subject matter and results, 2005

		Disposed of			
		After hearing			
	Set down for hearing	Allowed	Dismissed	Withdrawn or struck out	Total
Subject matter					
Bankruptcy:					
County courts	69	6	12	15	102
High Court Registrars	68	9	13	9	99
Total	**137**	**15**	**25**	**24**	**201**

Queen's Bench

In the Queen's Bench Divisional Court a total of 4,896 applications for leave to apply for judicial review were received in 2005. Over 13.8% of the total applications for leave to apply for judicial review dealt with in 2005 were allowed. During 2005, in immigration matters nearly 7.6% (219) of the 2,863 applications for permission determined were allowed, and in criminal and other matters just over 22.5% (458) of the total 2,033 applications for permission determined were allowed. Of the 263 substantive applications for judicial review disposed of in 2005, just over 42.6% (112) were allowed, over 54.4% (143) were dismissed and 3% (8) were withdrawn (see table 1.13).

Table 1.13
High Court – Queen's Bench Division – Administrative Court Matters: Applications for permission to apply for judicial review and applications for judicial review disposed of and results, 2005

	Applications for permission to apply for judicial review			Applications for judicial review disposed of					
				Determined by the Court					
				Single Judge		Divisional Court			
	Received	Granted	Refused	Allowed	Dismissed	Allowed	Dismissed	Withdrawn[1]	Total
Nature of review									
Immigration	2,863	219	1,349	24	36	–	–	1	61
Criminal	236	85	147	1	1	26	25	–	53
Others	1,797	373	671	61	77	–	4	7	149
Total	**4,896**	**677**	**2,167**	**86**	**114**	**26**	**29**	**8**	**263**

[1] The method for entering withdrawn matters on the database altered in 2000, therefore the withdrawn figures are lower than in the previous years

A total of 106 appeals by way of case stated were received in 2005, a decrease of 18.5% on the number received in 2004 (130). The vast majority, just over 79.2% (84), were appeals from magistrates' courts. Of the total number of 96 cases disposed of in 2005, over 46.9% (45) were allowed and (51) dismissed.

Table 1.14

High Court – Queen's Bench Division – Administrative Court Matters: Appeals by way of case stated received and disposed of and results, 2005

		Disposed of					
		Determined by the court					
		Single judge		Divisional Court			
	Total Received	Allowed	Dismissed	Allowed	Dismissed	Withdrawn	Total
Court or tribunal appealed from							
Crown Court	22	1	4	5	7	–	17
Magistrates' Court	84	16	13	23	27	–	79
Total	**106**	**17**	**17**	**28**	**34**	**-**	**96**

A total of 2,370 appeals and applications other than by way of judicial review and case stated were received in the Administrative Court during 2005, an increase of nearly 3.8% on the total number received in 2004. The increase is due to the effect of the new Statutory Review s.101 NIAA, 554 were concerned with statutory appeals. Of the total number of 1,941 cases disposed of in 2005, 21.2% (412) were allowed, over 78.6% (1,526) were dismissed (see table 1.15).

Table 1.15

High Court – Queen's Bench Division – Administrative Court Matters: Appeals and applications received and disposed of (other than by judicial review and case stated) and results, 2004

		Disposed of					
		Determined by the court					
		Single judge		Divisional Court			
	Total Received	Allowed	Dismissed	Allowed	Dismissed	Withdrawn	Total
Nature of appeal/application							
Statutory:							
Planning and related[1]	149	12	34	–	–	–	46
Others	391	74	38	13	32	3	160
Habeas Corpus	13	–	–	1	2	–	3
Committal for Contempt	1	–	–	1	–	–	1
Statutory Review S.101							
NIAA 2002	1,816	311	1,420	–	–	–	1,731
Total	**2,370**	**397**	**1,492**	**15**	**34**	**3**	**1,941**

[1] Includes appeal/applications under Town and County Planning Acts, Enforcement and Compulsory Purchase

Family

In the Family Division 5 appeals against orders made on domestic matters were disposed of in 2005. Of these, 2 were allowed and 1 dismissed, compared with 6 disposed of in 2004, when 2 were allowed and 4 dismissed. 2 appeals were dealt with were withdrawn or struck out (50% in 2004). Cases 'pending' for more than one year can also be dismissed at the discretion of the President of the Family Division.

During 2005, 54 appeals were made under section 94 of the Children Act 1989 and 12 were disposed of. Of these, one was allowed, 14 were dismissed, none were withdrawn or struck out.

Table 1.16
High Court – Family Division: Appeals set down and disposed of showing subject matter and results, 2005

		Disposed of			
	Set down	Allowed	Dismissed	Withdrawn or struck out	Total
Appeals to Divisional Court from orders made by magistrates' courts					
Domestic matters					
Adoption Act 1976	1	1	–	–	1
Section 33 of the Child Support Act	1	–	–	–	1
Domestic Proceedings/ Maintenance Orders	3	–	1	2	3
Family Proceedings Rules 1991	1	1			1
Appeals under Section 94 of the Children Act 1989 from orders made by Magistrates' Court	27	1	14	–	12
Total	**33**	**3**	**15**	**2**	**18**

Table 1.17

Appellate courts: Appeals entered in selected years since 1938, by nature of court

	1938	1958	1968	1978	1988	1998	2000	2001	2002	2003	2004	2005
Nature of court:												
Judicial Committee of the Privy Council	107	44	37	52	61	78	90	102	103	73	71	71
House of Lords:												
From Courts in England & Wales	32	29	41	77	75	77	63	80	243	228	208	73
Elsewhere	11	23	11	6	15	6	16	4	10	9	9	14
Court of Appeal:												
Civil Division	574	668	948	1,401	1,645	1,640	1,420	1,358	1,251	1,276	1,077	
Criminal Division[1]	..	..	6,414	6,099	7,235	8,649	7,740	7,440	7,718	7,451	7,591	7,023
High Court:												
Chancery Division	..	27	119	74	111	186	147	107	145	120	152	137
Queens Bench Division[2]	263	186	394	510	1,800	5,215	4,734	5,293	5,947	6,899[4]	6,619[4]	7,372[4]
Family Division	..	102	263	247	240	19	12	13	62[3]	60[3]	50[3]	33[3]
Total	**987**	**1,079**	**8,227**	**8,466**	**11,182**	**15,870**	**14,222**	**14,397**	**15,479**	**16,116**	**15,777**	**14,723**

[1] Includes applications

[2] Includes judicial review, appeals by way of case stated and statutory appeals

[3] Includes appeals under s94 Children Act 1989

[4] Includes Statutory Review s.101 NIAA

High Court – Chancery Division

In England and Wales civil justice is administered mainly by the county courts (Chapter 4) and the High Court, the latter handling the more substantial and complex cases.

The Chancery Division of the High Court comprises the Lord Chancellor, the Vice-Chancellor (its Head for practical purposes) and 17 High Court judges.

Although there is some overlap with the Queen's Bench Division, certain matters are specifically assigned to the Chancery Division. The principal business of the Division comprises corporate and personal insolvency disputes, business, trade and industry disputes, the enforcement of mortgages, intellectual property matters, copyright and patents, disputes relating to trust property and contentious probate actions.

Most Chancery business is dealt with in the Royal Courts of Justice in London and in eight provincial High Court centres which have Chancery jurisdiction.

During 2005 –

- the total number of proceedings started decreased by nearly 4% to 34,125 **(Table 2.1)**
- bankruptcy petitions issued in London increased by nearly 14% to 13,149 **(Table 2.5)**
- the number of company winding up petitions decreased by 23% to 6,276 **(Table 2.7)**

Chancery Division: Proceedings commenced, 1995-2005

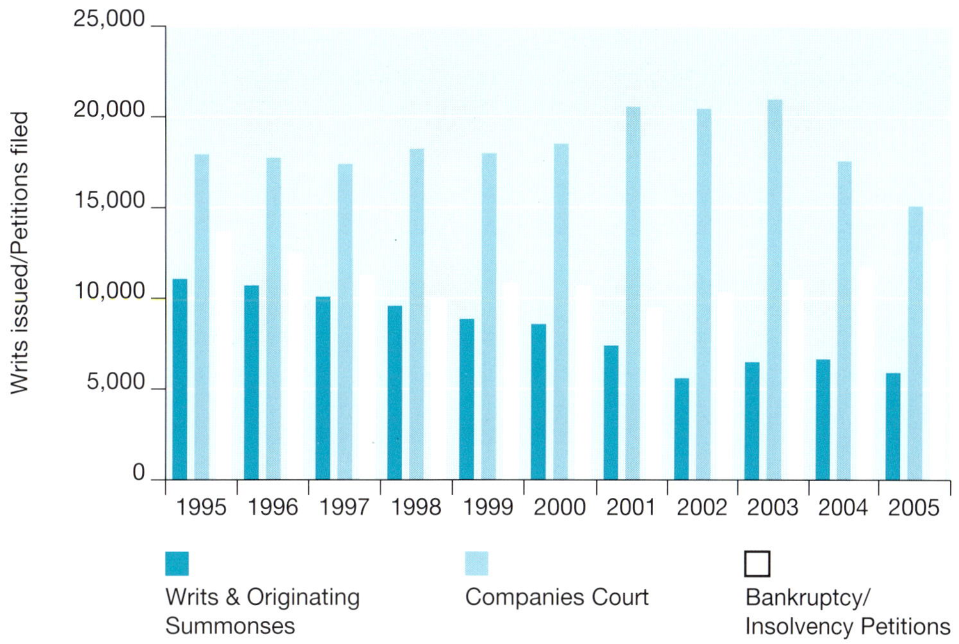

Chancery

Most actions begin with the issue of a claim or originating proceedings by the claimant against the defendant and are disposed of without a trial. Before an action comes to trial there may be a number of interlocutory hearings which are heard by judges and masters (in London) and district judges (outside London). Both masters and district judges are appointed by the Lord Chancellor and are solicitors or barristers of at least seven years standing. Trials come before High Court judges or deputy High Court judges (i.e. approved practitioners, retired High Court judges or circuit judges).

In 2005 there was a decrease of some 7% in the number of claims and originating proceedings issued in London, from 4,533 in 2004 to 4,219; of these, disputes over land accounted for nearly 16.5%. In dealing with this work in 2005, masters in London held 6,358 appointments in chambers (5,306 in 2004).

Table 2.1
Chancery Division: Matters dealt with in chambers by masters in London, 2005

Nature of proceedings	
Claims and other originating proceedings issued:	
London	4,219
Outside London[1]	1,672
Bankruptcy petitions	13,149
Companies Court proceedings[2]:	
London	11,571
Outside London	3,508
Patents Court appeals received	6
Total	**34,125**

Without Notice

[1] Contains an estimated 171 originating summonses

[2] Exluding transfers from the Chancery Division

Table 2.2
Chancery Division: Matters dealt with in chambers by masters in London, 2005

Orders made by masters[1]:	
Drawn up by drafting section	7,560
Not drawn up	1,982
Drawn up by solicitors	33
Transfers Out:	301
Enforcement Issues:	
Possession	39
Writs of fi-fa	53
Appointments before the masters:	
On notice	5,438
Without Notice	920

Table 2.3
Chancery Division: Claims and originating proceedings issued in London by nature of proceedings, 2005

Nature of proceedings	
Land:	
Contracts of sale and purchase	31
Landlord and Tenant	2
Mortgages and charges	12
Squatters and trespassers	–
Restrictive covenants	1
Other Proceedings	788
Business and industry:	
Partnership	41
Business fraud claims	1
Contracts of sale & purchase of shares & business	28
Other Disputes	716
Intellectual property:	
Confidential information	11
Passing off and trade marks	105
Patents and registered designs[1]	54
Copyright and design right[1]	148
Professional negligence:	
Claims against solicitors	52
Claims against accountants	1
Claims against surveyors and estate agents	–
Claims against members of other professions	13
Trusts, wills and probate:	
Contentious probate actions	115
Disputes relating to Trust property	27
Variation of Trusts	8
Inheritance (provision for dependants)	15
Guardianship of minors' estate	–
Charities	–
Other applications concerning wills and trusts	318
Other:	
Other debts, damages and accounts	1,701
Revenue appeals	16
Solicitors	15
Originating process not otherwise classified	–
Total	**4,219**

Table 2.4
Chancery Division: Cases listed in London, set down and disposed of, 2005

	Number of cases set down	Cases disposed of: After trial or hearing	Otherwise[1]	Total
Trial list	728	290	428	**718**
General list	235	116	127	**243**
Interim hearing list[2]	3,032	2,454	580	**3,034**
Total	**3,995**	**2,860**	**1,135**	**3,995**

[1] Settled out of court

[2] Now also includes the Interim Applications List

Bankruptcy

Bankruptcy is a term applied to insolvency (inability to pay debts) of individuals. Proceedings are started with a petition for bankruptcy. Although a debtor may issue his own petition it is more usual for a creditor to do so. Bankruptcy work is carried out in the High Court at the Royal Courts of Justice and in those county courts with bankruptcy jurisdiction (see chapter 4 for more information).

The number of bankruptcy petitions issued in the High Court in London during 2005 increased by nearly 12% to 13,149(11,533 in 2004). The total number of bankruptcy petitions filed in the High Court and the county courts during 2005 was, at 57,674, over 30% more than in 2004.

Table 2.5
Chancery Division: Bankruptcy petitions issued[1], 2005

Petitions issued	
By creditors	10,339
By debtors and legal representatives of deceased debtors	2,810
Total	**13,149**

During 2005, other applications dealt with by the registrars and administratively (mainly to set aside statutory demands, for interim orders, transfers and summonses) increased by 16% to 10,895.

Table 2.6
Chancery Division: Summary of bankruptcy proceedings before registrars[1] under the Insolvency Act 1986, 2005

Nature of proceedings	
Applications filed:	
Bankruptcy petitions by creditors	10,339
Bankruptcy petitions by debtors	2,810
Other applications and summonses	10,895
Total applications	**24,044**
Number of appointments before registrars:	
Listed	24,740
Unlisted	10,490
Orders made:	
Bankruptcy orders on creditors' petitions	4,411
Bankruptcy orders on debtors' petitions	2,795
Total orders made	**7,206**
Withdrawn/dismissed	5,692
Transfers to county courts	3,029
Orders	18,630

Companies Court

The Companies Court in London deals predominantly with the compulsory liquidation of companies and other matters under the Insolvency Act 1986 and Companies Acts. Unlike an individual, a company cannot be made bankrupt but may, because of insolvency or if there is some other reason it should cease to exist, be wound up instead. In addition to winding up proceedings, the Court exercises other powers in relation to registered companies. For example, a company can only reduce its capital with the approval of the Court. The Court also deals with an increasing number of claims to prevent individuals from being a director, liquidator, administrator, receiver or manager of a company or to take part in the running of a company under the Company Directors Disqualification Act 1986.

Most proceedings in the Companies Court are dealt with by registrars but certain applications are heard by judges. The Birmingham, Bristol, Cardiff, Leeds, Liverpool, Manchester, Newcastle-upon-Tyne and Preston District Registries have concurrent jurisdiction with the Companies Court in London.

The overall number of originating proceedings started in the Companies Court in London and the above district registries outside London in 2005 (15,079) was 13% less than in 2004. Orders made fell by nearly 16% to 18,848. 50% (7,530) of proceedings started were company winding up petitions; in London they rose by 7% to 4,749 and outside London they fell by over 33% to 2,781. Overall, winding up petitions remained steady. Winding up petitions in the High Court and the county courts during 2004 totalled 10,211.

Table 2.7
Chancery Division: Summary of Companies Court proceedings[1], 2005

	London	Outside London	Total
Applications filed:			
Winding–up petitions	4,749	2,781	**7,530**
Other petitions, applications and summonses	6,822	727	**7,549**
Orders made:			
On winding–up petitions:			
Winding–up orders made	1,924	887	**2,861**
Dismissed/Withdrawn	2,387	1,028	**3,415**
On other petitions, applications and summonses	10,171	386	**10,557**
Transfers to county courts	1,228	787	**2,015**
			18,848
Applications before registrar:			
Listed	12,395	2,278	**14,673**
Unlisted	435	262	**697**

Table 2.8
Chancery Division: Petitions for winding up by the Court presented at centres outside London

Centre	2005
Birmingham CJC	368
Bristol	1,969
Cardiff	4
Leeds	246
Liverpool	26
Manchester	144
Newcastle-upon-Tyne	24
Preston	0
Total	**2,781**

Patents Court – 2005

The Patents Court deals only with matters concerning patents, registered designs and appeals against the decision of the Comptroller General of Patents. Cases suitable to be heard by a county court are dealt with at the Central London County Court.

The Patents Court diary and judgment can be found on the internet at www.hmcourtservice.gov.uk together with a list of all trials and applications set down for hearing.

37 actions, which included trials and appeals, were listed. Of these 12 were withdrawn due to settlement or by order resulting from an interlocutory hearing. The hearings took about 88 court days, not taking into account pre-reading or judgment writing time.

82 interlocutories, which included case management conferences, applications for directions, summary judgment, applications to strike out etc, were listed and 31 withdrawn by consent. In the majority of cases of those withdrawn the terms of the order sought were agreed by the parties. The average time for this type of hearing is 1 hour and the total time taken throughout the year is about 20 court days.

7 appeals against the decision of the Comptroller General of Patents were listed. The total time taken in court was about 6 court days.

High Court – Queen's Bench Division

The Queen's Bench Division deals mainly with civil actions in contract and tort (civil wrongs) and also hears more specialist matters, such as applications for judicial review.

At the end of 2005 the Queen's Bench Division comprised the Lord Chief Justice(its President) and 72 High Court judges.

It contains within it the Commercial Court and the Admiralty Court (dealing with shipping matters such as damage to cargo and collision of ships) and administers the Technology and Construction Court (formerly the Official Referees Court) which hear cases involving prolonged examination of technical issues, such as construction disputes.

Judges of the Queen's Bench Division also hear the most important criminal cases in the Crown Court (Chapters 6 and 9) and they also sit in the Employment Appeals Tribunal (Chapter 7).

Queen's Bench Division work is dealt with at the Royal Courts of Justice in London and at district registries of the High Court, located at many of the county courts throughout England and Wales. Each registry covers a defined district consisting of one or more county court districts.

Queen s Bench Division: Writs & Originating Proceedings issued, 1995-2005

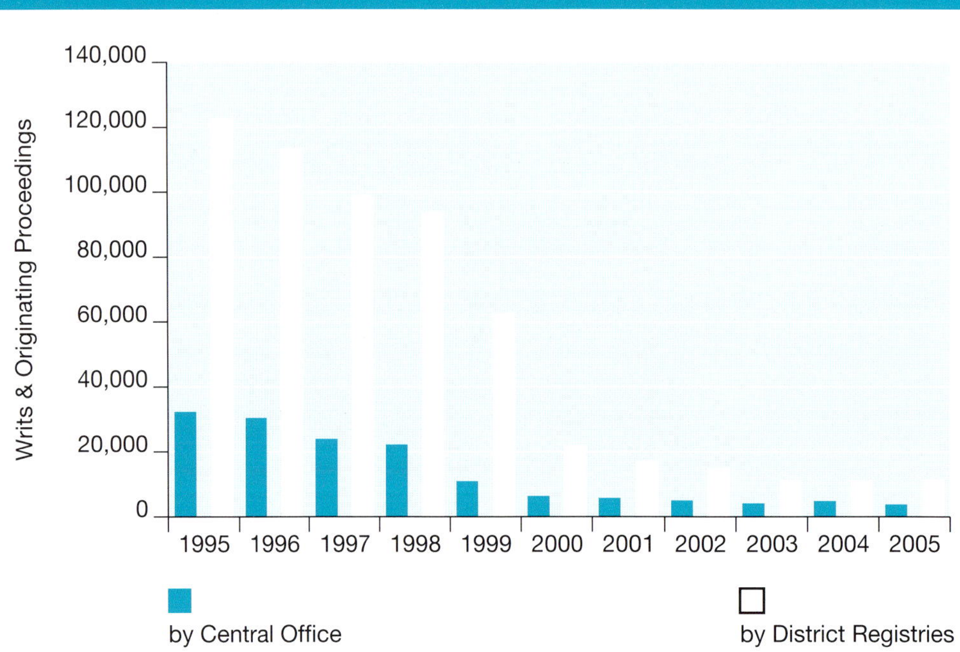

Queen's Bench

The Queen's Bench Division deals with common law business, that is, actions relating to contract (except those specifically allocated to the Chancery Division – see Chapter 2) and tort. Examples of contract cases dealt with in the Queen's Bench Division are failure to pay for goods and services and breach of contract. There are several types of tort (civil wrongs) including wrongs against the person only (e.g. defamation of character, libel) wrongs against property only (e.g. trespass) and wrongs which may be against people or property (e.g. negligence or nuisance). Some matters may involve both contract and tort, e.g. personal injury cases which show negligence and breach of a contractual duty of care. Others may be crimes as well as torts, for example assault.

Actions are normally started by way of a claim or an originating summons. A claim is the most common method and is used, for example, when a claim is based on an allegation of fraud or tort; it informs defendants what is claimed against them. An originating summons is used in certain cases, such as applications under specific Acts; it outlines the nature of the case. The hearing of an originating summons is usually before a master or district judge (for descriptions of masters and district judges see Chapter 2).

If a defendant fails to respond to a claim, a claimant may be entitled to a judgment in default. If a defendant responds any of the following may result –

a) the claimant discontinues the action

b) the parties settle (i.e. reach agreement)

c) the court decides that the defendant has no real defence to the action and gives summary judgment under order 14 of the Rules of the Supreme Court

d) a trial

There is a right of trial by jury for fraud, libel, slander, and malicious prosecution or false imprisonment cases. In all other cases the judge has discretion to allow trial by jury but it is only used exceptionally. A trial may result in an award of damages or a non-pecuniary remedy such as an injunction (an order to do or not do something). In jury trials the jury decides the amount of damages to be awarded.

Judgments may be enforced in many ways, the following being the most frequently used –

a) a writ of fieri facias (fi-fa) directing the sheriff (the equivalent of the bailiff in the county courts) by his officers to seize and if necessary sell the debtor's goods to raise money to pay off the debt

b) a writ of possession of land (eviction takes place if necessary to ensure that possession of property or land is recovered)

c) a writ of delivery of goods which is an order to hand over specific goods

d) a charging order on land, securities or funds in court (usually on land – this has the same effect as a mortgage, so that if the property is sold the amount of the charge (debt) must be paid out of the proceeds of the sale)

e) a garnishee order, which orders that a third party, normally a bank, holding money for the judgment debtor pay it to the judgment creditor direct

f) appointment of a receiver who will manage the judgment debtor's property or part of it in such a way as to protect the judgment creditor's interest in it

An order to attend court for questioning (formerly an oral examination) is a procedure used in connection with enforcement. The debtor is required to attend court to give details of his earnings, expenses, savings, etc., so that the creditor can decide how best to enforce the judgment. Often the debtor will pay before he can be questioned. Alternatively, a High Court judgment for money may be enforced in a county court as if it were a judgment of that court.

During 2005, 15,317 claims and originating proceedings were issued, 3.3% more than in 2004 (14,830).

Table 3.1
Queen's Bench Division: Proceedings started, 2005

Nature of proceedings	
Claims and originating summonses:	
Issued by Royal Courts of Justice	3,841
Issued by district registries[1]	11,476
Total	**15,317**

[1] Includes an estimated 1,195 originating summonses

In London 50% of claims were for an unliquidated amount of money and 32% were for amounts in excess of £50,000. 22.4% of claims were for debt and a further 18.6% were for personal injury.

Table 3.2
Queen's Bench Division: Proceedings started, 2005

Nature of claim	£15,000 – £50,000	Over £50,000	Unliquidated	Total
Claim for Debt (goods sold & delivered, work carried out etc)	256	380	227	**863**
Breach of contract	94	219	262	**575**
Clinical Negligence[2]	19	125	207	**351**
Personal Injury Actions	66	204	446	**716**
Other Negligence (inc. professional negligence)	17	59	121	**197**
Defamation (libel, slander)	43	70	139	**252**
Tort (eg. nuisance,trespass, assault wrongful arrest etc)	18	10	35	**63**
Recovery of land / property	–	–	14	**14**
Miscellaneous	159	171	480	**810**
Total	**672**	**1,238**	**1,931**	**3,841**

[1] Figures given are for the Royal Courts of Justice only

[2] Previous years data is not available

In London the number of judgments given either in default of a response by the defendant or as summary judgments during 2005 totalled 595, a decrease of 12.4% from 2004 (679).

Table 3.3
Queen's Bench Division-Judgment without trial: judgments by default and summary judgment (Under Order 14) by amount of judgment[1], 2005

Type of judgment	£15,000 – £50,000	Over £50,000	Unliquidated	Total
By default	210	246	119	**575**
Order (including order 14)	4	6	10	**20**
Total	**214**	**252**	**129**	**595**

[1] Figures given are for the Royal Courts of Justice only

Tables 3.4-3.9 on cases disposed of are not currently available. Contact Alan Sealy for more information

Although Queen's Bench Division cases are only tried at the Royal Courts of Justice and first tier centres outside London, interlocutory proceedings (applications preparatory or incidental to the main proceedings) are dealt with at all district registries and at the Royal Courts of Justice. This area of work decreased in 2005 – applications to masters in London decreased by 11.7% to 9,335. The court determines what, if anything, must be done before a case can be set down for trial, gives directions as to when this is to be done and where the trial is to take place. If either party is dissatisfied with an order of a master, an appeal may be made to a judge in chambers (a private hearing).

Table 3.10
Queen's Bench Division[1]: Applications for masters in London, 2005

Type of application	Total
For directions	–
Summary judgment (Order 14)	–
Other summonses	9,335
Total	**9,335**

During 2005, the number of enforcement proceedings issued in London decreased by 37.7% to 11,847. Writs of fi-fa formed nearly 98% of proceedings. Outside London enforcement proceedings decreased by 17.6% to 29,415, writs of fi-fa accounting for 99% of proceedings. Charging orders and garnishee orders absolute were the second and third most common methods of enforcement respectively.

Table 3.11
Queen's Bench Division: Enforcement proceedings issued, 2005

Nature of Enforcement	London	Outside London	Total
Writs of fi–fa	11,626	24,413	**36,039**
Writs of possession	22	–	**22**
Writs of Delivery	1	–	**1**
Charging orders	170	–	**170**
Garnishee orders absolute	28	–	**28**
Application for orders to attend court for questioning	–	2	**2**
Total	**11,847**	**24,415**	**36,262**

Admiralty Court

The Admiralty Court deals with shipping matters. The two most common matters dealt with are damage to cargo and collision of ships. Most cases are dealt with at the Royal Courts of Justice in London but some are disposed of in district registries with appropriate jurisdiction. There is one Admiralty Judge who hears all Admiralty cases and a number of interlocutory matters. The Judge is supported by the Admiralty Registrar who hears interlocutory matters and post judgment applications. The Admiralty Marshal is responsible for the detention and sale of ships which are the subject of proceedings in the Admiralty Court.

During 2005, there were 102 Admiralty actions started in the Royal Courts of Justice. Of the claims issued in London, 27 (26%) related to damaged cargo.

Table 3.12
Queen's Bench Division: Admiralty proceedings[1], 2005

Nature of proceedings	
Claims issued	102
Summonses issued:	
Judges	37
Registrars	47
Applications heard	84
References to registrar	2
Warrants of arrest executed[2]	22
Sales by the Court	1

[1] Figures are for the Royal Courts of Justice only

[2] Vessels or property arrested

Table 3.13
Queen's Bench Division: Admiralty claims issued showing nature of action[1], 2005

Nature of action	
Collision	19
Damage to cargo	27
Personal injury (including fatal)	5
Mortgage	2
Limitation of liability	1
Others	48
Total	**102**

[1] Figures are for the Royal Courts of Justice only

Table 3.14

Queen's Bench Division: Admiralty actions for trial in the High Court set down, tried or otherwise disposed[1], 2005

Actions for trial	
Set down during year	25
Tried during year	3
Otherwise disposed of	19

[1] Figures are for the Royal Courts of Justice only

Commercial Court

The Commercial Court also deals with shipping matters but is largely concerned with matters regarding contracts related to ships, insurance, carriage of cargo and the construction and performance of mercantile contracts. Other matters dealt with involve banking, international credit, contracts relating to aircraft, the purchase and sale of commodities and the practice of arbitration and questions arising from arbitrations. There are twelve Commercial Judges who hear all commercial cases and interlocutory applications.

During 2005, 798 (81.3%) of the 981 claims were unspecified. The majority of these (55%) were for breach of contract.

Table 3.15

Commercial Court: Claims issued showing nature and amount of claim[1], 2005

Nature of claim	Under £20,000	Over £20,000	Unspecified claims	Total
Claim for Debt (goods sold & delivered, work carried out etc)	3	6	8	**17**
Breach of contract	3	145	393	**541**
Miscellaneous	–	26	397	**423**
Total	**6**	**177**	**798**	**981**

[1] Figures given are for the Royal Courts of Justice only

Technology and Construction Court

The Technology and Construction Court, deals with building and engineering disputes and computer litigation. Other matters dealt with include sale of goods, valuation disputes, landlord and tenant (especially dilapidations), torts relating to the occupation of land and questions arising from arbitrations in building and engineering disputes.

The business of the court also includes any cases in the Chancery or the Queen's Bench Divisions which involve issues or questions which are technically complex or for which trial by such judges is in any reason desirable.

There are seven full-time circuit judges based in London assigned to the Supreme Court Group. They are nominated by the Lord Chancellor, and presided over by a resident High Court judge. Outside London, nominated circuit judges sit on each of the circuits with further full-time designated judges at Birmingham, Manchester and Liverpool.

Table 3.16
Technology and Construction Court: Actions received, tried and disposed of[1], 2005

Received:	
Claims and originating summonses issued in registry	274
By transfer	66
Total	**340**
Disposed of:	
Tried	3
Struck out, settled or discontinued	23
Transferred	18
Default judgments entered	7
Total	**51**
Number of summonses and interlocutory applications heard during year	496

[1] Figures are for the Royal Courts of Justice only

County Courts

There are currently 218 county courts in England and Wales that hear civil proceedings, which can be commenced in either county courts or the High Court.

Some county courts also handle family proceedings such as divorce, domestic violence and matters affecting children. Generally the High Court handles the more substantial, important and complex cases (Chapters 2, 3, and 5).

During 2005 –

- claims issued rose by 17.1% **(Table 4.1)**
- Mortgage possession orders made rose by 52.7% to 70,845 **(Table 4.6)**
- 47,521 claims were disposed of by way of small claims procedure **(Tables 4.8 & 4.9)**
- the average waiting period for a trial was 58 weeks between issue and trial **(Table 4.16)**
- creditors' and debtors' bankruptcy petitions rose by 36% **(Table 4.22)**
- company winding-up petitions entered rose from 1,56 to 1,801

County Court claims issued by amount of claim, 2005[1]

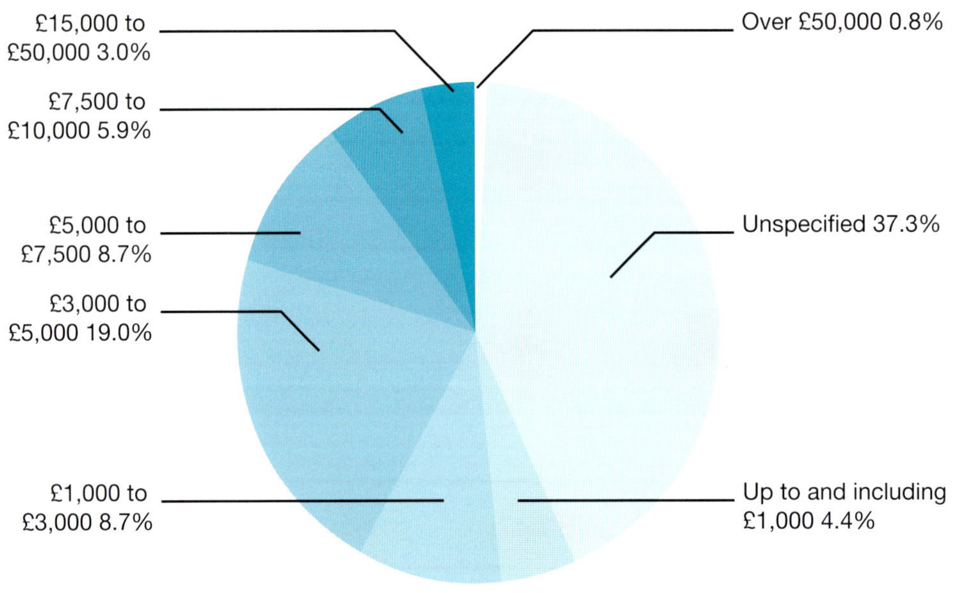

[1] Figures are based on three months sample data from selected county courts

Introduction

Since 1 July 1991 county courts have had jurisdiction to deal with all contract and tort cases and recovery of land actions within the appropriate areas of jurisdiction, regardless of value. In addition, all county courts may deal with the following types of proceedings –

a) certain equity and contested probate actions (for example, actions concerning an alleged breach of trust obligation by a trustee or questions concerning the administration of a will) where the value of the trust, fund or estate does not exceed £30,000

b) any action which all parties agree to have heard in a county court (e.g. defamation cases) except cases on certain aspects of trust, family and admiralty law

Some courts also hear –

a) divorce matters (see Chapter 5)

b) bankruptcy and insolvency matters

c) matters under the Race Relations Act 1976

Other than at the smallest courts, each county court is assigned at least one circuit judge and one district judge. Circuit judges generally hear cases worth over £15,000, or those involving greater importance or complexity. Claims between £5,000 and £15,000 are tried by either circuit or district judges. District judges hear small claims (in most instances, these are claims under £5,000), repossession claims and the assessment of damage awards in uncontested cases. District judges also case manage most of the cases proceeding in the county courts.

Claims and miscellaneous hearings

Starting a case
The normal method of taking someone to court is for the person doing so (the claimant) to complete a claim form and issue it at a county court. The claim can be issued in any county court. On receipt of the claim form the court allocates a claim number and enters the details into the court's records. A response pack is attached to the claim form which is then sent to (served on) the person being sued (the defendant). The defendant has a specific time limit in which to reply to the claim. During that time a defendant can either pay the claim, dispute it (defend it), admit the claim and ask for more time

to pay it or ignore it. If the claim is defended, a judge will allocate the claim to one of three tracks for case management purposes –

a) the small claims track – generally for cases with a value up to £5,000

b) the fast track – for cases with a value over £5,000 but less than £15,000

c) the multi-track – cases with a value in excess of £15,000

Each track involves a different degree of judicial involvement. Procedures in the small claims track are the most informal.

If a defendant does not reply to the claim, the claimant can ask the court to enter judgment, that is to make an order that the defendant pay the claim. If the defendant has admitted the claim and asks for more time to pay and the claimant accepts the offer, a request for judgment can similarly be made.

Should the judgment not be paid as the court has ordered, it is open to the claimant to issue enforcement proceedings to obtain payment. Judgments and enforcement are explained in more detail later in this chapter.

The Claim Production Centre

The Claim Production Centre (CPC) was set up in January 1990 to process claim requests received on magnetic media from major claimants – i.e. claimants who generally issue more than 1,000 claims annually. Issue and dispatch of claims is guaranteed within 24-48 hours. The CPC has customers such as banks, credit card and storecard issuers, mail order catalogues, utilities and solicitors specialising in debt recovery. It issued 938,571 claims representing 59.4% of the total default claims issued in 2005. Although located in Northampton, the CPC is deemed to be part of the court in whose name the claim is issued and once the claim is issued and served, that court will deal with the case in the usual way.

The 2005 figure of 1,580,511 (Table 4.2) claims entered represented an increase of 1% on the 2004 figure. Money claims issued represented 84.5% of the total. The remainder were fixed date actions, 89.7% of which were actions for the recovery of land, mostly relating to residential premises.

Table 4.1
Claims issued and warrants of execution[1] issued in selected years, 2005

Year	Money[1] claims[2]	Claims for the recovery of land[3]	Total	Warrants of execution against goods issued
	Claims issued			
2001[4]	1,478,360	243,356	1,721,716	394,414
2002	1,386,418	242,139	1,628,557	374,020
2003	1,347,414	227,178	1,574,592	355,157
2004	1,364,866	232,257	1,597,123	309,521
2005	1,610,347	260,027	1,870,374	339,259

[1] For years prior to 1978 figures relating to the Mayor's and City of London Court are not included

[2] From 1988 includes unliquidated claims

[3] From 1990 does not include Order 24 originating applications

[4] The data extraction method has changed, please see chapter 11 for further details

Table 4.2
Summary of proceedings started, 2005

Nature of proceedings	
Claims entered:	
'Money' claims	
Default actions	1,580,511
Fixed date actions (other than for possession)	29,836
Actions for possession of land	260,027
Bankruptcy petitions	44,525
Companies Act:	
Winding-up petitions	7,350
Family matters (major areas of work)[1]:	
Adoption applications (originating)	3,111
Divorce, nullity and judicial separation petitions	152,782

[1] For details of these and other family matters dealt with by county court see Chapter 5

Table 4.3
Main proceedings started by region, 2005

	Default actions[1]		Fixed date actions[2]	
Region	Number	%	Number	%
London	92,037	6	65,661	23
Midlands	114,067	7	50,036	17
North East	109,483	7	38,298	13
North West	110,516	7	34,702	12
South East	133,431	8	54,323	19
South West	83,767	5	26,739	9
Wales and Cheshire	43,362	3	20,104	7
Bulk Centres	893,848	57	–	–
England & Wales	**1,580,511**	**100**	**289,863**	**100**

[1] Including claims issued by the Claim production Centre

[2] Including actions for possession of land (except those under Order 24 of the County Court Rules)

[3] Referred to later in this chapter

Table 4.4
Default actions: Claims issued by Claim Production Centre, 2005

Region	Number
London	5,874
Midlands	3,666
North East	1,248
North West	1,809
South East	18,975
South West	8,329
Wales and Cheshire	4,822
Bulk Centres	893,848
Money Claim Online (MCOL)	66,087
England & Wales	**938,571**

[1] Referred to later in this chapter

Recovery of Land

The total number of actions started for recovery of land rose from 232,257 in 2004 to 260,027 in 2005. Mortgage possession actions increased by 48.7% from 77,574 in 2004 to 115,353. Of the total number of mortgage possession actions issued in 2005, over 99% concerned private mortgages and the remainder, local authorities. During 2005, a total of 70,845 mortgage possession orders were made, of which 53.2% were suspended.

Table 4.5
Recovery of Land: Actions entered and orders made for recovery of land by type of action, 2005[3]

Local authority mortgage possessions:	
Actions entered	280
Suspended orders made	11
Orders made	82
Other mortgage possessions:	
Actions entered	115,073
Suspended orders made	37,688
Orders made	33,064
Other possession actions by social landlords[1]:	
Actions entered	126,306
Suspended orders made	56,833
Orders made	29,088
Other possession actions by private landlords[2]:	
Actions entered	18,368
Suspended orders made	2,212
Orders made	9,821
	428,826

[1] Includes actions by local authorities and housing associations

[2] Includes actions by all landlords except local authorities and housing associations

[3] The data extraction method has changed, please see chapter 11 for further details

Table 4.6
Recovery of Land: Mortgage possession actions[1], years since 2001

		2001	2002	2003	2004	2005
Local Authority	Actions entered	986	419	633	282	280
Actions	Orders made[2]	78	129	194	82	93
Other Mortgage	Actions entered	66,462	63,729	66,396	77,574	115,072
Possession Actions	Orders made[2]	47,751	41,150	40,488	46,327	70,751
Social Landlord	Actions entered	155,419	158,783	141,681	137,190	126,306
Possession Actions	Orders made[2]	105,098	107,864	96,620	92,952	85,931
Private Landlord	Actions entered	20,489	19,208	18,468	17,210	18,368
Possession Actions	Orders made[2]	12,491	12,032	11,701	10,631	12,034

[1] Including suspended orders

[2] The data extraction method has changed, please see chapter 11 for further details

Judgments and hearings

Judgment can be entered in various ways in county courts. Most of the judgments in money claims are entered by default (i.e. in the absence of a response from the defendant within the allotted 14 days from the date of service of the claim) or by the claimant accepting the defendant's offer to pay all or part of the amount claimed. There is generally no need to involve either a circuit judge or a district judge in these cases. However, they become involved when there is a defence against all or part of the claim and the matter is set down for a trial or a small claims hearing. Fixed date actions can also lead to trials.

On 26 April 1999, the limit for small claims increased from £3,000 to £5,000 for all claims except personal injury which remained at £1,000 and housing disrepair for which the limits are £1,000 for the disrepair and £1,000 for damages. The increase has widened the value band of cases which are automatically referred to the small claims track when a defence is filed.

Table 4.7
Defences Made and allocated by track in each region, 2005

Region	Defences Made	Allocation to track: Small Claims	Fast-Track	Multi-Track	Total allocations to Track
London	34,185	12,849	7,983	5,117	25,949
Midlands	32,261	12,331	8,606	4,811	25,748
North East	31,576	10,412	9,215	5,072	24,699
North West	43,953	8,357	9,872	4,951	23,180
South East	34,272	17,948	7,261	4,538	29,747
South West	24,279	11,103	4,839	3,528	19,470
Wales & Cheshire	13,369	5,242	4,572	2,098	11,912
England & Wales	213,895	78,242	52,348	30,115	160,705

Table 4.8
Proceedings disposed of by trial or claim hearing by region, 2005

	Trials		Small Claims	
Region	Number	%	Number	%
London	3,970	23	9,240	19
Midlands	2,298	13	6,835	14
North East	2,432	14	5,704	12
North West	3,069	18	4,838	10
South East	3,037	18	12,053	25
South West	1,117	6	5,860	12
Wales and Cheshire	1,395	8	2,991	6
England & Wales	**17,318**	**100**	**47,521**	**100**

Table 4.9
Proceedings disposed of by small claim, by nature of claim and by region, 2005

Region	Personal injury	Other negligence	Debt	Non-possession housing disputes	Other	Total
London	1,988	1,279	4,836	317	820	9,240
Midlands	488	740	4,766	58	783	6,835
North East	432	447	4,333	32	460	5,704
North West	932	434	2,862	103	507	4,838
South East	1,351	1,521	8,260	109	812	12,053
South West	409	396	4,462	86	507	5,860
Wales and Cheshire	400	246	2,026	26	293	2,991
England & Wales	**6,000**	**5,063**	**31,545**	**731**	**4,182**	**47,521**

Table 4.10
Small claims heard by nature of claim, type of claimant and defendant, 2005[1]

	Claimant				Defendant			
Nature of claim	individual	firm	corp	Total	individual	firm	corp	Total
Debt	*40.2*	*13.9*	*23.0*	*77.1*	*45.0*	*15.7*	*16.4*	*77.1*
Negligence – personal injury	*1.8*	*0.1*	–	*1.9*	*1.5*	*0.1*	*0.3*	*1.9*
Other negligence	*10.9*	*0.4*	*1.3*	*12.7*	*8.5*	*1.2*	*3.0*	*12.7*
Non possession housing dispute	*0.4*	*0.1*	–	*0.5*	*0.5*	–	–	*0.5*
Other	*6.4*	*0.4*	*0.9*	*7.8*	*3.8*	*1.2*	*2.8*	*7.8*
Total	***59.8***	***14.9***	***25.3***	***100***	***59.3***	***18.3***	***22.4***	***100***

[1] Figures in italics are weighted estimates based on three months sample data from selected county courts

Table 4.11
Small Claims heard by nature of claim and award, 2005[1]

Nature of claim	non monetary	£1k or less	£1k –£3k	£3k –£5k	Over £5k	Total
Debt	*14.1*	*24.8*	*26.3*	*9.4*	*2.5*	*77.1*
Negligence – personal injury	*0.5*	*0.7*	*0.6*	*0.1*	–	*1.9*
Other negligence	*2.5*	*4.0*	*4.9*	*1.2*	*0.1*	*12.7*
Non possession housing dispute	*0.1*	*0.1*	*0.1*	*0.2*	-	*0.5*
Other	*2.0*	*2.4*	*2.4*	*0.5*	*0.5*	*7.8*
Total	***19.2***	***32.0***	***34.3***	***11.5***	***3.1***	***100***

Table 4.12

Average waiting and hearing times for small claims, by nature of claim, 2005[1]

Nature of claim	Average waiting time in weeks (issue of claim to start of small claims)	Average length of small claim (minutes)
Debt	*25*	*68*
Negligence – personal injury	*25*	*63*
Other negligence	*25*	*79*
Non possession housing dispute	*34*	*153*
Other	*24*	*69*
Total	***25***	***70***

Table 4.13

Trials by nature of claim and whether civil funding granted[1], 2005

		Civil funding granted for			
	Number of cases	Both parties	Claimant only	Defendant only	Neither party
Debt	*17.3*	*3.6*	*4.3*	*4.0*	*12.6*
Negligence – PI	*58.0*	*12.9*	*18.2*	*13.3*	*39.4*
Other negligence	*6.0*	*1.2*	*1.4*	*1.2*	*4.5*
Other	*18.6*	*3.4*	*5.2*	*4.0*	*12.9*
Total	***100***	***21.0***	***29.2***	***22.4***	***69.5***

[1] All figures in italics are weighted estimates based on two months sample data and may not add up due to rounding

Table 4.14

Actions set down for trial[1], disposed of and results by nature of claim, 2005

	Method of disposal				Result of action after attending court			
	Attending court							
	After trial	Settled during hearing	Struck out	Total	For claimant	For defendant	For both	Total
Debt	*13.8*	*2.4*	*1.2*	*17.3*	*14.4*	*2.3*	*0.6*	*17.3*
Negligence – PI	*43.6*	*10.5*	*3.9*	*58.0*	*43.7*	*12.1*	*2.2*	*58.0*
Other negligence	*4.8*	*0.8*	*0.3*	*6.0*	*4.0*	*1.5*	*0.7*	*6.2*
Other	*13.3*	*4.0*	*1.4*	*18.6*	*15.1*	*1.9*	*1.5*	*18.6*
Total	***75.7***	***17.7***	***6.7***	***17,320***	***77.2***	***17.8***	***5.1***	***100***

[1] All figures in italics are weighted estimates based on two months sample data and may not add up due to rounding

Table 4.15
Trials disposed of[1] by amount of award and nature of claim, 2005

	Monetary award								
	< £1k	£1 – 3k	£3 – 5k	£5 – 7.5k	£7.5 – 10k	£10k – 50k	> £50k	Non monetary	No. of cases
Debt	*1.0*	*0.7*	*2.8*	*2.4*	*1.7*	*3.8*	*0.6*	*4.4*	*17.3*
Negligence – PI	*2.6*	*6.8*	*13.8*	*5.0*	*3.5*	*5.3*	*2.0*	*19.0*	*58.0*
Other negligence	*0.3*	*0.5*	*1.4*	*0.7*	*0.2*	*0.5*	*0.5*	*1.9*	*6.0*
Other	*0.5*	*0.8*	*0.9*	*0.7*	*0.5*	*2.4*	*1.0*	*12.0*	*18.6*
Total	***4.4***	***8.7***	***19.0***	***8.7***	***5.9***	***11.9***	***4.1***	***37.3***	***100***

[1] All figures in italics are weighted estimates based on two months sample data and may not add up due to rounding

Table 4.16
Trials disposed of[1] by type of judge and average length of hearing, by nature of claim, 2005

	Heard by				
	Circuit judge	District judge	Deputy District judge	No. of cases	Average length of hearing
Debt	*8.74*	*8.12*	*0.50*	*17.35*	3 Hours 35 Mins
Negligence – PI	*28.87*	*23.42*	*5.70*	*57.99*	3 Hours 23 Mins
Other negligence	*2.91*	*2.29*	*0.87*	*6.07*	4 Hours 12 Mins
Other	*11.40*	*6.20*	*0.99*	*18.59*	4 Hours 31 Mins
Total	***51.92***	***40.02***	***7.99***	***100***	**3 Hours 40 Mins**

[1] All figures in italics are weighted estimates based on two months sample data and may not add up due to rounding

Table 4.17
Average waiting times[1] for the trials by centre and nature of claim, 2005

	between issue & allocation	between allocation & trial	between issue & trial
Debt	25	29	54
Negligence – PI	29	22	51
Other negligence	18	30	48
Other	24	29	53
London:	25	27	52
Debt	22	74	96
Negligence – PI	22	29	51
Other negligence	19	31	50
Other	27	28	54
Outside London:	23	36	59
England & Wales	**23**	**35**	**58**

[1] Figures are based on two months sample data and may not add up due to rounding

Table 4.18
Registry of County Court Judgments: Judgments registered, satisfied, cancelled and searches carried out, 2005

	2005
between issue & set down	19
between set down & trial	31
between issue & trial	50

Registration of judgments

Registry Trust Ltd (a private non-profit making company limited by guarantee) administers the Register of County Court Judgments, a statutory public register originally set up 150 years ago. Entries on the Register can be cancelled when a judgment is set aside, reversed or is paid in full within a month. Judgments paid in full after a month can be noted on the Register as satisfied. All entries are automatically removed at the end of the sixth calendar year after the date of judgment. The Register is open for public inspection, on payment of a statutory fee, and is used in particular by credit reference agencies to assist lenders in making responsible credit granting decisions, for the benefit of both consumers and businesses. During 2005, 1,018,886 judgments were registered, 31.9% more than in 2004. The number of judgments satisfied or cancelled in 2005 was 195,207, a 3.3% rise against the number in 2004. From April 2006, a new Register of Judgments Orders and Fines will come into effect, containing High Court judgments and magistrate's court fines, in addition to county court judgments and administration orders.

Table 4.19
Registry of County Court Judgments: Judgments registered, satisfied, cancelled and searches carried out during the 1st Quarter 2005.

Judgments:	
Registered	1,018,886
Satisfied	108,919
Cancelled	86,288
Searches:	
Postal	14,995
Personal	3,449
Internet	5,812

Enforcement of judgments

Warrants of execution

There are various methods of enforcing judgments in county courts. The most common method is the warrant of execution against a debtor's goods, where, unless the amount due under the warrant is paid, saleable items owned by a debtor can be sold. During 2005, 339,341 such warrants were issued, a rise of 9.6% over 2004. The number of warrants issued for possession of land rose by 10.7% to 131,505, and the number of warrants executed (possession taken) rose from 50,493 to 57,729.

The County Court Bulk Centre

The County Court Bulk Centre (CCBC) was set up in March 1992, initially to process the work of 'distributed' claimants who, until the venue rule change in July 1991, had issued in all or most county courts. The CCBC is a central processing unit, attached to Northampton County Court, and is designed to relieve the courts of the routine repetitive tasks associated with processing large volumes of debt recovery cases, such as entry of judgment and issue of warrants of execution. The CCBC provides a service for entry of judgment and warrant production for major claimants who between them issued 893,848 claims through the Claim Production Centre during 2005. The CCBC also entered 646,435 judgments (increase by 44% on 2004) and issued 209,121 warrants of execution (a increase of 85% on 2004).

Money Claim Online (MCOL), the Court Service's first online service, was launched in February 2002. The service enables claimants to issue claims over the Internet to recover money owed to them by logging on to www.courtservice.gov.uk/mcol. The claimant pays the court fee by credit or debit card. Claims are issued in the name of Northampton County Court. Claimants can view the progress of their claim online and, where appropriate, the user can request entry of judgment and issue a warrant of execution online. The scope of MCOL was extended in January 2003 to enable both MCOL and CCBC defendants to reply to a claim online. MCOL is now issuing more claims than any local county court and issued 66,087 claims in 2005 compared to 51,910 in 2004.

Traffic Enforcement Centre

The Traffic Enforcement Centre (TEC) enables authorities which have de-criminalised on-street parking to collect penalty charges through the civil courts in the name of Northampton County Court. TEC also deals with unpaid penalty charges relating to vehicle emissions and, for London, fixed penalties for the encroachment of bus lanes. 2003 saw the introduction of London Congestion Charging and this also impacted on TEC for registration of unpaid penalty charges. During 2005 TEC received a total of 1,630,718 registrations and authorised the issue of 1,369,240 warrants of execution, which were processed by certificated bailiffs.

Charging orders

In order to obtain security for payment of a judgment or order, rather than to obtain the money itself, a creditor (the person to whom the debt is owed) may impose a charge on the debtor's property, for example on the debtor's house. Should the debtor later sell the property the creditor is assured of receiving some money before most other claims are met. This is called a charging order. Once a charging order has been made absolute a claimant may apply for an order for sale. The number of applications for charging orders issued in 2005 rose by 44.1% to 65,676.

Third Party Debt Orders (previously known as Garnishee orders)

Third Party Debt Orders previously known as Garnishee orders , are a method of enforcement used by creditors to secure the payment of an outstanding judgment debt by freezing then seizing money owed or payable by a third party to a debtor in order to pay the judgment debt. The debts targeted are usually within deposit-taking institutions such as banks and building societies. The number of garnishee / third party debt orders rose in 2005 by 3.1% to 6,593.

Table 4.20
Enforcement proceedings, 2005[1]

Nature of proceedings	
Warrants of execution against goods issued	339,341
Warrants of delivery of goods	2,380
Warrants of possession of land:	
Issued	131,505
Executed	57,729
Interpleader summonses	275
Judgment summonses issued	64
Third part debt orders issued	6,593
Charging order applications issued	65,676

[1] The data extraction method has changed, please see chapter 11 for further details

Attachment of earnings orders

Another common method of enforcement is for a creditor to obtain an attachment of earnings order which obliges the debtor's employer to deduct a set sum from the debtor's pay and forward it to the court. The number of applications to secure payment of a debt in this way increased by 22% in 2005 to 91,949. Orders made as a result of such applications were 0.3% more than in 2004. Applications to secure payment of maintenance during 2005 decreased by 12.2% to 613.

Table 4.21
Enforcement proceedings: Proceedings under the Attachment of Earnings Act 1971, 2005

Nature of proceedings	
To secure payment of maintenance:	
Applications	613
Orders made[1]	601
To secure payment of a judgment debt:	
Applications	91,949
Orders made[2]	40,923

[1] Includes re-direction and discharge of orders

[2] Includes re-direction of orders

[3] The data extraction method has changed, please see chapter 11 for further details

Administration orders and Orders to obtain information from judgment debtors(previously known as oral examinations)

In certain circumstances a debtor may combine his debts into an administration order. The debtor must have a judgment debt and at least one other which he is unable to pay. The total indebtedness should not exceed £5,000. Once the debts have been examined and found to be correctly calculated a district judge can make an order for the debtor to make regular payments to the court. The court will then distribute the money in the appropriate proportions to the creditors listed by the debtor. 3,700 administration orders were granted in 2005, over 5% less than in 2004

Changes to the oral examination procedure were introduced on 26 March 2002. The name was changed to orders to obtain information from judgment debtors and the process was streamlined and standardised to enable information to be obtained faster. Orders to obtain information from judgment debtors are used to assist the claimant in determining the most appropriate method of enforcing a judgment; it is not a method of enforcement. However, the fact that debtors will be ordered to attend court to provide details of their means often results in the debtor paying the debt. The debtor has to provide information such as income, expenditure, employment and bank accounts. A total of 32,098 orders were made for orders to obtain information from judgment debtors in 2005.

Bankruptcy and company winding-up

A person or company with debts which they are unable to pay is called insolvent. When speaking about individuals the term bankrupt is used to indicate insolvency. Proceedings in insolvency are presently regulated by the Insolvency Act 1986. Proceedings start when either a creditor or debtor issues a bankruptcy or companies petition. Proceedings may be started at county courts with the appropriate jurisdiction or in the Chancery Division of the High Court. The total of 44,525 bankruptcy petitions issued during 2005 was 36% more than in 2004.

Table 4.22
Bankruptcy petitions issued[1], 2005

By creditors	10,438
By debtors or by legal representatives of deceased debtors	34,087
Total	**44,525**

[1] See also Table 2.5 (High Court – Bankruptcy)

When it becomes necessary to bring to an end a company's existence, whether due to insolvency or for some other reason, the process is called 'winding-up'. There is a restriction on proceedings that may be started in county courts based on the paid-up capital of the company to be wound up; most winding-up work is commenced and carried out in the Chancery Division of the High Court at the Royal Courts of Justice and at eight provincial centres. County courts issued 4,569 petitions for winding-up in 2005, compared with 1456 in 2004 (see Chapter 2 for overall trends in company winding-up petitions).

Family Matters

Family matters are dealt with in the Family Division of the High Court, in county courts and, with the exception of divorce proceedings, in family proceedings courts (those parts of magistrates' courts having a family jurisdiction).

Most matters affecting children are dealt with under the Children Act 1989 in all three levels of courts.

Contentious probate matters are dealt with in the Chancery Division of the High Court (Chapter 2).

During 2005 –

- Children Act applications in public law cases decreased by 1% **(Table 5.1)**
- the number of residence orders made in private law proceedings fell by 12% and contact orders made rose by over 18% **(Table 5.3)**
- adoption orders decreased by over 15% to 3,867 **(Table 5.4)**
- 151,654 petitions were filed for divorce, a decrease of over 10% **(Table 5.6)**

Dissolution of Marriage: Petitions Filed and Decree Nisi Granted, 1995-2005

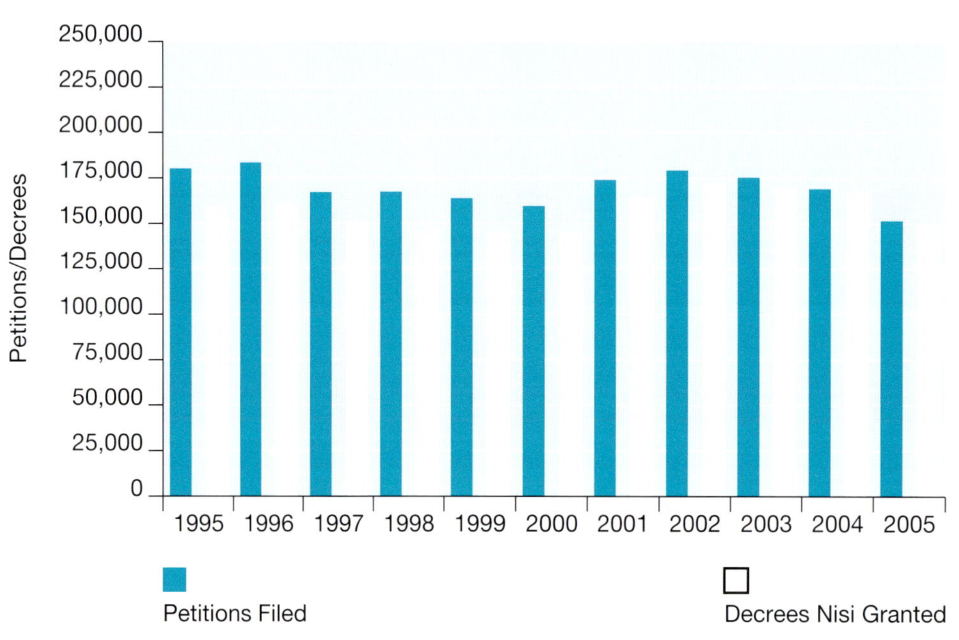

The Children Act 1989

Courts' jurisdiction
The Children Act 1989, which was implemented in October 1991, established for the first time a concurrent family jurisdiction across all tiers of court, including the family proceedings courts.

County Courts
County courts were given five different types of jurisdiction –

i) non-divorce county courts which have no family jurisdiction

ii) divorce county courts which can issue all private law family proceedings, contested matters being transferred to family hearing centres for trial

iii) family hearing centres which can issue and hear all private law family cases whether or not they are contested

iv) care centres which have full jurisdiction in private and public law matters

v) Specialised Adoption Centres, which have jurisdiction to issue, process and hear adoption applications under guidance issued by the President of the Family Division

Public law cases are those usually brought by local authorities or the NSPCC and include matters such as care, supervision and emergency protection orders.

Private law cases are those brought by private individuals, generally in connection with divorce or the parents' separation.

The High Court
The High Court has jurisdiction to hear all cases relating to children and exercises an exclusive jurisdiction in wardship. The High Court also hears appeals from family proceedings courts and cases transferred from the county courts or family proceedings courts. The Family Division of the High Court consists of the President and 17 High Court judges. High Court work is dealt with at the Principal Registry of the Family Division (PRFD) in London and in the provinces by those district registries which have divorce jurisdiction.

Family Proceedings Courts
Family proceedings courts' work is dealt with by lay magistrates and sometimes by district judges (magistrates' courts) sitting with lay colleagues. The lay magistrates sitting at these courts are drawn from a specially selected family panel and have had to undertake special and ongoing training. The district judges (magistrates' courts) are also specially trained. Family proceedings courts have full private and public law jurisdiction under the Act although they do not deal with divorce cases.

Judges' and magistrates' jurisdiction

In order to hear proceedings under the Children Act 1989 in the county courts, judges must be specially nominated for family work by the Lord Chancellor. These judges receive special family work guidance. Circuit judges not so nominated may still hear matrimonial and domestic violence injunctions –

- district judges can hear private law family work but have a limited jurisdiction (district judges of the PRFD have full private law and public law jurisdiction)
- nominated care district judges have increased jurisdiction and can hear uncontested public law cases and contested private law cases
- circuit family judges have full private law jurisdiction but do not deal with public law cases
- nominated care judges have full public and private law jurisdiction
- designated family judges also have full jurisdiction in public and private law: based at care centres, they also chair local Family Court Business Committees and Family Court Forums
- lay magistrates and district judges (magistrates' courts) hear cases in both public and private law

Applications

Proceedings under the Children Act are started by application in the manner prescribed by the Family Proceedings Rules 1991 (for county courts and the High Court) and the Family Proceedings Courts (Children Act 1989) Rules 1991 (for family proceedings courts). Public law cases must start in the family proceedings court but may be transferred up to the county court –

- to minimise delay
- to consolidate with other family proceedings
- where the matter is exceptionally grave, complex or important

Private law cases can commence at any family proceedings court or county court. Cases can also be transferred laterally between courts.

During 2005 a total of 22,160 public law applications were made (a increase of less than 1% from 2004) and 101,063 private law applications (a decrease of over 6%) were made.

Table 5.1
Public and Private law applications[1,4] made in each tier of court by circuit, 2005

	Public Law				Private Law			
Circuit	FPC[2]	CC[3,4]	HC	Total	FPC[2]	CC[4]	HC	Total
PRFD	–	843	54	897	–	5,276	150	**5,426**
London	2,987	–	–	2,987	2,278	6,917	–	**9,195**
Midlands	2,713	927	18	3,658	3,890	12,783	23	**16,696**
North East	1,786	2,482	109	4,377	2,363	13,851	33	**16,247**
North West	1,506	859	33	2,398	2,389	10,385	21	**12,795**
South East	2,295	1,930	4	4,229	1,993	19,417	11	**21,421**
South West	1,399	801	9	2,209	1,191	10,870	44	**12,105**
Wales and Cheshire	717	662	26	1,405	879	6,289	10	**7,178**
England & Wales	**13,403**	**8,504**	**253**	**22,160**	**14,983**	**85,788**	**292**	**101,063**

[1] Some inconsequential applications have been excluded

[2] Figures in italics are weighted estimates based on data received from a number of family proceedings courts, and may not add up due to rounding

[3] The county court public law applications are not comparable with those published in previous years due to a change in the method of collection. They no longer include cases that have been transferred from Family Proceedings courts

[4] Applications are ALL applications made in this year. County Court Care and supervision applications for interim care and supervision orders

Disposal of applications
There are four ways in which an application can be disposed of –

i) withdrawn applications: can only be withdrawn by order of the court

ii) order refused: in public law proceedings an order is refused if the grounds are not proved and the court has dismissed the application. In private law proceedings the court may refuse to make an order or make an order of no order

iii) order of no order: this is made if the court has applied the principle of non-intervention under section 1(5) of the Act. This provides that the court shall not make an order unless it considers that doing so would be better for the child than not making the order at all

iv) order made

Orders

The Act provides a wide range of orders which can be made according to the child's best interests. Below are some typical orders.

Care/Supervision Orders

On an application from a local authority or authorised person (at present only the NSPCC), if the court is satisfied that a child is suffering, or is likely to suffer, significant harm and that the harm or likelihood of harm is attributable to (i) the care given to the child or the likelihood of the care not being what it would be reasonable to expect a parent to give a child, or (ii) where the child is beyond parental control, the court may make an order –

a) placing the child in the care of a designated local authority

b) putting the child under the supervision of a designated local authority or probation officer

No care or supervision order may be made in respect of a child who has reached the age of 17 (or 16 in the case of a child who is married). The effect of a care order is to impose a duty on the local authority to keep a child in care, have parental responsibility for the child and (subject to certain provisions under the Act) determine the extent to which a parent or guardian may meet his or her parental responsibility for the child. While a supervision order is in force, it is the duty of the supervisor to advise, assist and befriend the child and take the necessary action to give effect to the order including whether or not to apply for its variation or discharge.

Emergency Protection Orders

A court may make an emergency protection order if it is satisfied that there is reasonable cause to believe that a child is suffering, or is likely to suffer, significant harm if not removed to accommodation provided by the applicant or does not remain in the place he or she is presently living. Anyone, including a local authority, can apply for an emergency protection order if, for example, they believe that access to the child is being unreasonably refused.

Exclusion Requirements

In October 1997 changes to the Children Act gave courts the power to order the exclusion of the suspected abuser from the child's home in cases where ill-treatment of a child is alleged, and either an Interim Care Order (ICO) or Emergency Protection Order (EPO) is made. (Previously, the child would usually have been removed.)

The court can add a power of arrest to the 'exclusion requirement'.

Where exclusion is ordered, there must be a person remaining in the property with the child. That person must agree to care for the child and consent to the exclusion requirement.

Section 8 orders
Orders made under section 8 of the Act are frequently sought for –

- residence (where the child should live)
- contact (whom the child sees)
- prohibited steps (to prevent an action being taken)
- specific issue (about a specific aspect of the child's upbringing)

It is always preferable that agreement between the parents about arrangements for the children be reached rather than an order having to be imposed. During 2005 a total of 97,432 section 8 orders were made in private law, a decrease of almost 16% on 2004.

Table 5.2
Disposal of selected application type in public law in all tiers of court, 2005

Nature of application[3]	Applications made	Applications withdrawn	Orders refused	Orders of no orders	Orders made
FPC:					
Care	9,146	201	10	92	2,133
Contact with a child in care	277	92	16	65	213
Discharge of care	434	130	22	15	320
Refusal of contact	391	44	7	7	453
Emergency protection order	2,530	327	39	29	2,097
Secure accommodation	428	65	7	9	475
Supervision	567	33	0	7	826
Supervision order – discharge	52	7	1	0	45
Section 8:					
Residence	283	58	12	3	733
Contact	90	22	21	7	134
Prohibited steps	15	5	0	0	24
Specific issue	20	1	5	0	13

Table 5.2
Disposal of selected application type in public law in all tiers of court, 2005 *continued*

Nature of application	Applications made	Applications withdrawn	Orders refused	Orders of no orders	Orders made
CC:					
Care	3,610	87	3	136	4,371
Contact with a child in care	448	34	5	20	186
Discharge of care	1,088	69	7	7	478
Refusal of contact	734	8	0	0	1,012
Emergency protection order	171	13	0	2	133
Secure accommodation	69	0	0	0	144
Supervision	299	12	0	2	1,636
Supervision order – discharge	3	0	0	0	0
Section 8:					
Residence	864	39	5	2	1,691
Contact	899	43	5	32	1,328
Prohibited steps	36	0	0	0	166
Specific issue	138	9	0	0	124
HC:					
Care	99	11	1	9	161
Contact with a child in care	15	0	0	0	5
Discharge of care	21	0	0	0	23
Refusal of contact	23	0	0	0	28
Emergency protection order	3	4	0	0	6
Secure accommodation	10	0	0	0	29
Supervision	9	0	0	0	101
Supervision order – discharge	5	0	0	0	0
Section 8:					
Residence	31	2	0	0	69
Contact	29	1	0	1	87
Prohibited steps	0	0	0	0	23
Specific issue	4	0	0	0	7

Table 5.2

Disposal of selected application type in public law in all tiers of court, 2005 *continued*

Nature of application	Applications made	Applications withdrawn	Orders refused	Orders of no orders	Orders made
Total by type:					
Care	12,855	299	14	237	6,665
Contact with a child in care	740	126	21	85	404
Discharge of care	1,543	199	29	22	821
Refusal of contact	1,148	52	7	7	1,493
Emergency protection order	2,704	344	39	31	2,236
Secure accommodation	507	428	7	9	648
Supervision	875	45	0	9	2,563
Supervision order – discharge	60	7	1	0	45
Section 8:					
Residence	1,178	99	17	5	2,493
Contact	1,018	66	26	40	1,549
Prohibited steps	51	5	0	0	213
Specific issue	162	10	5	0	144
Total by court type:					
FPC	14,233	986	139	234	7,466
CC	8,359	314	25	201	11,269
HC	249	18	1	10	539
Total	**22,841**	**1,318**	**165**	**445**	**19,274**

1 Contains imputed data for family proceedings courts

2 Not all applications made in 2005 had a disposal in 2005, so the number of disposals will not be the same as the number of applications

3 Applications are only shown by the application categories above in this year, so will be slightly lower than the number of applications in Table 5.1. County Court Care and supervision applications may include some applications for Interim Care and Supervision Orders

Table 5.3
Disposal of selected applications type in private law in all tiers of courts, 2005[2]

	Applications made	Applications withdrawn	Orders refused	Orders of no orders	Orders made
FPC					
Parental responsibility	3,394	599	180	63	2,489
Section 8:					
Residence	4,054	610	121	61	3,408
Contact	5,982	1,350	321	231	4,455
Prohibited steps	417	113	22	20	181
Specific issue	503	100	47	13	361
County Court					
Parental responsibility	7,516	215	15	251	6,194
Section 8:					
Residence	26,940	685	24	599	22,564
Contact	28,641	992	58	2,088	54,762
Prohibited steps	9,733	180	19	151	7,929
Specific issue	6,760	182	7	124	2,887
High Court					
Parental responsibility	5	0	0	5	38
Section 8:					
Residence	94	9	0	11	194
Contact	68	7	0	23	452
Prohibited steps	44	7	0	8	93
Specific issue	58	5	1	6	55
Totals					
Parental responsibility	10,915	814	195	319	8,721
Section 8:					
Residence	31,088	1,304	145	671	26,166
Contact	34,691	2,349	379	2,342	59,669
Prohibited steps	10,194	300	41	179	8,203
Specific issue	7,321	287	55	143	3,303

[1] Applications are only shown by the application categories above in this year, so will be slightly lower than the number of applications in Table 5.1

[2] Not all applications made in 2005 had a disposal in 2005, so the number of disposals will not be the same as the number of applications

'The Voice of the Child'

On the 1st April 2001, the Lord Chancellor became responsible for the Children and Family Court Advisory and Support Service (CAFCASS). With effect from 12th January 2004 the Lord Chancellor's responsibilities for CAFCASS were transferred to the secretary of state for the Department for Education and Skills. This new organisation brings together the work of three existing court advisory services –

- the Family Court Welfare Service
- the Guardian ad Litem (GAL) and
- the Reporting Officer Panels and the Children's Division of the Official Solicitors Office

Amalgamating the work of each of the above services now provides an improved service to the courts, better safeguards regarding the interests of children, reduces wasteful overlaps and so increases efficiency.

CAFCASS advises the courts on issues such as placing children in local authority care, applications regarding section 8 orders. Examples are residence, contact, or prohibited steps order to prevent a child being taken abroad.

What it will mean for us in the Family Courts

As a consequence, some of the family court staff's job titles have changed –

- the term Guardian ad Litem is replaced with the new term Children's Guardian
- Guardian ad Litem (in Human Fertilisation cases) becomes Parental Order Reporter
- Welfare Officer remains unchanged except in cases that involve appointments under section 7(1)(a) of the Children Act. In this case the term welfare officer will change to Children and Family Reporter
- finally, the term Reporting Officer remains unchanged

Children's Guardian

The court will appoint a Children's Guardian for the child in specified proceedings (broadly, public law proceedings) unless satisfied that it does not need to do so in order to safeguard the child's interests. The role of the Children's Guardian includes ensuring that the court is fully informed of the relevant facts which relate to the child's welfare and that the wishes and feelings of the child are clearly established.

The new service will combine the family court welfare service currently provided by the Probation Service, the Children's branch of the Official Solicitor's Department and local authority Guardian ad Litem and Reporting Officer services. They are all described as officers of CAFCASS.

The Welfare Officer
The welfare officer plays a very significant role in private law proceedings (a children's Guardian cannot be appointed in such proceedings). He or she is responsible for providing the court with information about matters relating to the welfare of the child which enables the court to make decisions which are in the child's best interests. As part of that process the welfare officer has particular regard to the wishes and feelings of the child concerned. The welfare officer may also have a role to play in helping the parents or other adults closely concerned with the child to reach agreement about issues which are in dispute and thus avoid the need for a contested court hearing. National Standards for Probation Service Family Court Welfare Work came into effect on 1 January 1995.

Protocol for Judicial Case Management in Public Law Children Act Cases
The 1st November 2003 saw the introduction of the protocol for Judicial Case Management in Public Law Children Act Cases. Delay in care cases has been identified as one blot on the otherwise successful implementation of the Children Act 1989.

The protocol sets a guideline of 40 weeks for the conclusion of care cases. Some cases will need to take longer than this, but many more cases should take less.

The aim of the Protocol is to reduce delay and improve the quality of justice for children and families by –

- Proper court control of proceedings
- Identifying and promoting best practice
- The consistent application of best practice by all courts
- Providing predictable standards which the courts will treat as the normal and reasonable approach to the conduct of proceedings by parties

Other Child Matters

Wardship

Wardship is where the court assumes responsibility for the welfare of a child and exercises parental responsibility. Only the High Court can order that the child be made or cease to be a ward of court. Under the Children Act, the use of wardship by local authorities is severely limited and leave to make an application for any exercise of the court's inherent jurisdiction must be granted by the High Court. The Act does not affect applications made by private individuals but the same result could generally be achieved by obtaining a prohibited steps order or a specific issue order under section 8. Care orders in respect of wards of court will bring that wardship to an end. Those wardships that had not been returned to the High Court for a further application by 14 October 1992, i.e. during the transitional period allowed for by the Children Act, were generally treated as discharged.

Adoption

An adoption order made by a court extinguishes the rights, duties and obligations of the natural parents or guardian and vests them in the adopters. On adoption the child becomes for virtually all purposes in law the child of its adoptive parents and has the same rights of inheritance of property as any children born to the adoptive parents. Before issuing an adoption order the court must be satisfied that –

a) the adoptive parent(s) are suitable and consent to the adoption

b) the consent of the natural parent(s) has been obtained (after October 14 1991 it became necessary to obtain the consent of each parent or guardian with parental responsibility for the child)

The court may dispense with the natural parents' consent if, for example, a parent has persistently ill-treated the child or the court takes the view that the adoption order is in the child's best interests and consent is being unreasonably withheld. The court's first consideration is to safeguard and promote the welfare of the child, taking into account the child's views (having regard to their age and understanding) and giving them due consideration.

During 2005, 3,867 orders for adoption were made (a decrease of over 10%). Of these, 20% (800) were made to step-parents, 3% less than in 2004 (when 1,040 of the 4,539 orders were to step-parents).

Table 5.4
Adoption of children: Summary of proceedings, 2005

Nature of proceedings	Family proceedings courts[1]	County Courts	High Courts	Total
Applications:				
By step–parents	483	440	0	**923**
By others	973	2,671	4	**3,648**
Total	**1,456**	**3,111**	**4**	**4,571**
Orders made:				
to step–parents	381	416	3	**800**
to others	741	2,276	50	**3,067**
Total	**1,122**	**2,692**	**53**	**3,867**

[1] Contains imputed data for family proceedings courts

Matrimonial Matters

Divorce

There are two ways to dissolve a marriage. The most usual is a decree absolute of divorce, which ends a valid marriage. The other is a decree of nullity, which declares that the marriage itself is void, i.e. no valid marriage ever existed, or voidable, i.e. the marriage was valid unless annulled. No petition may be made for divorce within the first year of marriage.

To obtain a decree of divorce the marriage must be proved to have broken down irretrievably. This must be done on proof of one or more of the following facts –

a) adultery

b) behaviour with which the petitioner cannot reasonably be expected to live

c) desertion of at least two years

d) two years separation where the respondent consents

e) five years separation without consent

Nullity

A void marriage is one that is legally invalid because, for example –

a) either party was under the age of sixteen at the time of the marriage

b) either party was already married

c) the parties are prohibited from marrying, for example father and daughter

Examples of voidable marriages are those –

a) not consummated due to incapacity or wilful refusal (most nullities are on these grounds)

b) where one party was suffering from a venereal disease in a communicable form, or was pregnant by someone else at the time of marriage

Judicial Separation
An alternative to divorce is a decree of judicial separation. This does not dissolve the marriage but absolves the parties from the obligation to live together. This procedure might, for instance, be used if religious beliefs forbid or discourage divorce.

Procedure
The procedure is for one party (the petitioner) to petition for divorce, nullity or judicial separation. A district judge considers the evidence and, in divorce and nullity cases, if the grounds are proven, a decree nisi, which is a provisional measure, will be made. Six weeks later the petitioner can apply for a decree absolute, which is the final measure. Alternatively the respondent (i.e. the other party) can apply a further three months later. Only when the decree absolute has been issued by the court can either party remarry. For judicial separation, a district judge considers the evidence and makes a (final) decree for judicial separation, there being no provisional stage. In most cases of divorce or separation all the proceedings are dealt with in the county court. However, if the case is of sufficient complexity, difficulty or gravity it can be transferred to the High Court. It is also usual for the High Court to hear cases when it is already dealing with proceedings between the couple, especially where the interests of children are involved, for instance, where children of the family might still be the subject of wardship proceedings.

Where the couple has children, the court has to be satisfied with the arrangements for their welfare. The arrangements have to be submitted in writing and will, if possible, have been agreed by both parents. However, both the petitioner in the divorce and the respondent may file alternative proposals. If the district judge is dissatisfied in any way with the arrangements made for the child (e.g. because of conflict in counter proposals issued by the parties) then the district judge may order the parents to appear in order to resolve the issues. At this appointment the district judge may, if the issues are uncontested, consider making a section 8 order.

During 2005 petitions for divorce fell by over 10% to 151,654 (167,193 in 2004). Petitions filed for nullity decreased by 12% to 436 while petitions for judicial separation fell by just over 7% to 692. Divorce decrees nisi fell by 9% to 150,668 and absolute fell by 7% to 142,393. Separation decrees granted decreased by just over 8% to 387 (419 in 2004).

Table 5.5

Matrimonial suits: Summary of proceedings in selected years since 1938

	1938	1958	1968	1978	1988	1998	2002[1]	2003	2004	2005
Dissolution of marriage:										
Petition filed	9,970	25,584	54,036	162,450	182,804	165,870	177,223	173,240	167,193	151,654
Decrees nisi	7,621	23,456	47,959	151,533	154,788	144,231	170,966	167,992	166,042	150,668
Decrees absolute	60,692	22,195	45,036	142,726	152,139	141,543	147,465	154,284	153,689	142,393
Nullity of marriage:										
Petition filed	263	655	971	1,117	604	505	443	463	492	436
Decrees nisi	170	496	819	959	389	281	216	204	308	257
Decrees absolute	158	459	758	941	494	267	186	193	244	251
Judicial Separation:										
Petition filed	71	158	233	2,611	2,925	916	1,001	826	742	692
Decrees granted	25	88	105	1,228	1,917	519	560	467	419	387

[1] The data extraction method has changed, please see chapter 11 for further details

Table 5.6

Matrimonial suits: Petitions filed and decrees granted by circuit, 2005[2]

	Petitions Filed			Decree Nisi		
Circuit	Divorce	Nullity	Judicial separation	Divorce	Nullity	Judicial separation[1]
London	13,450	94	76	12,915	50	35
Midlands	26,349	78	105	26,255	45	54
North East	22,518	44	116	23,018	31	68
North West	16,015	40	71	15,704	24	49
South East	34,245	90	122	33,884	56	68
South West	21,154	41	62	21,191	30	37
Supreme Court Group	6,879	37	73	6,849	13	42
Wales and Cheshire	11,044	12	67	10,852	8	34
England & Wales	**151,654**	**436**	**692**	**150,668**	**257**	**387**

[1] Final decrees

[2] The data extraction method has changed, please see chapter 11 for further details

Maintenance

In many matrimonial cases where there are no children to the marriage no formal order for financial provision (ancillary relief) is sought by either party. It is more common for maintenance to be sought where there are children and the Children Act gave a wide range of powers to all tiers of court in this respect. Under the Child Support Act 1991, which came into force on 5 April 1993, the courts lost a substantial part of their jurisdiction to make orders for child maintenance (although they may still make orders for spousal maintenance). This work is instead being handled by the Child Support Agency, which operates its own collection and enforcement service for child maintenance assessments. It can make orders for maintenance to be deducted from earnings and can apply to magistrates' courts for a range of enforcement action. Orders for financial provision are not dependent upon divorce proceedings and may be made for children (these have also been affected by the Child Support Act).

During 2005 15,468 maintenance orders in respect of children, 9,470 lump sum and 10,946 property adjustment orders were made in the county courts (15,612, 9,470 and 11,673 in 2004, respectively).

Table 5.7

Matrimonial suits: Orders made for ancillary relief, under the Matrimonial Causes Act 1973, in the county courts, 2005[1]

Nature of Enforcement	By Consent	Contested	Total
Periodical Payments	1,322	3,399	**4,721**
Maintenance Pending Suit	613	442	**1,055**
Application Dismissed	672	1,141	**1,813**
Lump Sum Orders	1,948	7,522	**9,470**
Lump Sum Orders	2,548	8,398	**10,946**
Pension Sharing or Attachment Orders	830	2,113	2,943
Secure Provision Order	454	1,023	**1,477**
Above orders made for child	3,503	11,965	**15,468**

[1] The data extraction method has changed, please see chapter 11 for further details

Enforcement of Maintenance

In some cases payments of maintenance are not made as ordered and action can be taken to enforce payment. This is usually done by using the enforcement procedures available in magistrates' courts. If the order was originally made in the county court, the person due to receive the money may apply to the county court to have the maintenance order registered in the magistrates' court for collection. Where the payer is employed, it is also possible to apply for an order from the county court for payments to be taken direct from their salary. These are called attachment of earnings orders. Magistrates' courts can also make similar orders for deductions from pay. The final sanction used to make someone comply with certain civil orders (including matrimonial) is to order their committal to prison for contempt of court. Usually the threat of this is sufficient but occasionally it will result in arrest and imprisonment. These powers have been modified by the Child Support Act 1991 which transfers certain functions to the Child Support Agency, which has enhanced enforcement powers.

During 2005, 1,033 applications to have maintenance orders registered in magistrates' courts were granted in the county courts, just under 9% more than in 2004. In addition, 639 attachment of earnings orders were made.

Table 5.8

Matrimonial suits: Enforcement proceedings in the county courts, 2005[2]

Nature of enforcement proceedings	
Attachment of earnings orders on maintenance orders:	
Applications made	654
Orders made[1]	639
Registration of maintenance orders in magistrates' courts:	
Orders made	1,033

[1] Includes discharge orders

[2] The data extraction method has changed, please see chapter 11 for further detail

Domestic Violence

Part IV of the Family Law Act provides single and unified domestic violence remedies in the magistrates' courts and the county courts. Two types of order can be granted: a non- molestation order, which can either prohibit particular behaviour or general molestation; and an occupation order, which can define or regulate rights of occupation of the home.

A range of people can apply to the court: spouses, cohabitants, ex-cohabitants, those who live or have lived in the same household (other than by reason of one of them being the other's employee, tenant, lodger or boarder), certain relatives (e.g. parents, grandparents, in-laws, brothers, sisters), and those who have agreed to marry one another.

Where the court makes an order and it appears to the court that the respondent has used or threatened violence against the applicant or child, then the court *must* attach a power of arrest unless it is satisfied that the applicant or child will be adequately protected without such a power.

The court may also add an exclusion requirement to an emergency protection order or interim care order made under the Children Act 1989. This means a suspected abuser may be removed from the home, rather than the child, as was previously the case.

Table 5.9

Family Law Act 1996 – part IV: Domestic Violence applications and orders made in the county courts, 2005[1]

Nature of proceedings	
Non-Molestation - ex parte	13,037
Non-Molestation - on notice	4,303
Occupation - ex parte	6,817
Occupation - on notice	3,166
Applications for warrants for arrest	13
Warrants for arrest issued	107
Remainds in custody	598
Remands on bail	256
Remands medical	7

[1] The data extraction method has changed, please see chapter 11 for further details

Protection from Harassment Act 1997
New legislation was introduced in two stages to provide protection to victims of harassment. In June 1997, implementation of section 3(1) and (2) came into force. These allow civil proceedings to be taken against anyone pursuing a course of harassment and may result in the grant of injunction, an award of damages, or both.

In September 1998, the remainder of section 3 came into force. The effect of this in the civil courts was to make breach of a civil injunction enforceable by warrant of arrest.

Probate

Following the wider spread of home and share ownership, it is becoming increasingly necessary either to obtain probate of a will or letters of administration (if there is no will) when someone dies. The power of the executor to administer the estate comes from the terms of the will itself but in other cases distribution may only be possible once a grant of probate or administration has been issued. This enables the asset holders to release the accounts of the deceased to the person named in the grant.

The Family Division deals with all cases of non-contentious (uncontested) probate. If the validity of the will is challenged, the Chancery Division has jurisdiction to hear such applications. There are 12 Probate Registries in England and Wales: 10 District Probate Registries in various locations throughout England, the Probate Registry of Wales and the Principal Registry in London.

In 2005 there were 299,215 grants of representation issued (294,018 in 2004). Of these, there were 86,349 personal applications and 212,866 made by solicitors. In 212,046 of these cases the deceased left a will.

Table 5.10

High Court Family Division – Probate: Grants in non–contentious proceedings issued, re-sealed and revoked, 2005

Nature of application	On personal Application	On Application by Solicitors	Total
Probates:			
Principal Registry	9,404	3,945	**13,349**
District Probate Registries[1]	49,850	133,508	**183,358**
Letters of Administration with will annexed:			
Principal Registry	806	300	**1,106**
District Probate Registries[1]	3,816	8,193	**12,009**
Letters of Administration:			
Principal Registry	2,906	3,207	**6,113**
District Probate Registries[1]	16,788	61,295	**78,083**
Total	**83,570**	**210,448**	**294,018**
Grants revoked	–	–	**297**
Grants re–sealed	–	–	**527**
Standing Searches	–	–	**1,053**

[1] The figures for individual registries are available on application to the Principal Probate Registry

The Crown Court

The Crown Court, which sits at 92 locations in England and Wales, deals with criminal matters including –

- cases for trial by magistrates' courts in respect of 'indictable only' offences (i.e. those which can **only** be heard by the Crown Court)
- 'either way' offences (i.e. those which can be heard in either a magistrates' court or the Crown Court)
- defendants committed from magistrates' courts for sentence
- appeals against decisions of magistrates' courts

During 2005 –

- total receipts for committals for trial increased by 1% to 80,021 and disposals decreased by over 5% to 77,175 **(Table 6.2)**
- cases dealt with where a plea of guilty was recorded increased by over 1% to 41,578 **(Table 6.8)**
- the average waiting time for defendants on bail was nearly 16 weeks and 14 weeks for those held in custody (just over 16 and 14 weeks respectively in 2004) **(Table 6.18)**
- receipts of committals for sentence increased by nearly 6% to 32,937, while appeals fell by less than 1% to 12,809 **(Tables 6.12 and 6.13)**

Crown Court: Committals for trial, 1995-2005

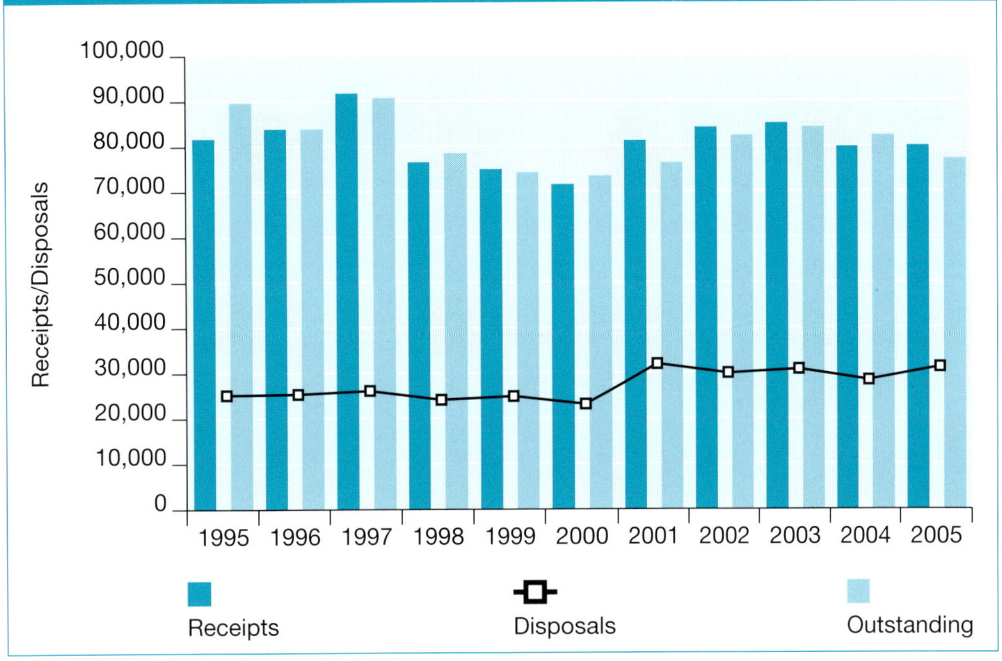

Introduction

The Crown Court is the only court which has jurisdiction to hear criminal trials on indictment and it also exercises the appellate and other jurisdictions which had been exercised, prior to its establishment in 1972, by Quarter Sessions. It is a unitary court but currently sits at 92 centres throughout England and Wales. Court centres are of three kinds. First-tier centres are those visited by High Court judges for Crown Court work, and also for High Court civil business. Second-tier centres are those visited by High Court judges for Crown Court business, but not for civil business. Third-tier centres are those not normally visited by High Court judges at all. Circuit judges and recorders may sit at all three classes of centre to deal with Crown Court cases.

Committals for Trial

For the purpose of trial in the Crown Court, offences are divided into four classes of seriousness according to directions given by the Lord Chief Justice, with the concurrence of the Lord Chancellor –

- **Class 1.** These are the most serious offences and are generally to be tried by a High Court judge unless a particular case is released on the authority of a Presiding judge to a circuit judge. The offences include treason and murder.

- **Class 2.** These offences are generally also to be tried by a High Court judge unless a particular case is released on the authority of a Presiding judge to a circuit judge or other judge. The offences include manslaughter and rape.

- **Class 3.** These may be listed for trial by a High Court judge, but may be tried by a circuit judge or recorder if the listing officer, acting under the directions of a judge, so decides. Class 3 offences include all offences triable only on indictment other than those specifically assigned to classes 1, 2 and 4, for example, aggravated burglary, kidnapping and causing death by dangerous driving.

- **Class 4.*** These offences are normally tried by a circuit judge or recorder, although they may be tried by a High Court judge. They include grievous bodily harm, robbery and conspiracy, and all 'either way' offences** – those which may be tried either on indictment at the Crown Court or summarily (i.e. in a magistrates' court).

  *From 6 June, the above method of classifying offences was amended and class 4 was omitted. All former class 4 offences now fall into class 3 category.

  In a Practice Direction which amended the Consolidated Criminal Practice Direction handed down by the Lord Chief Justice on 8 July 2002, the following is to apply with effect from 6 June 2005.

Class 1:

a) Misprision of treason and treason felony
b) Murder
c) Genocide
d) Torture, hostage taking and offences under the War Crimes Act 1991
e) An offence under the Official Secrets Acts
f) Manslaughter
g) Infanticide
h) Child destruction
i) Abortion (section 58 of the Offences against the Person Act 1861)
j) Sedition
k) An offence under section 1 of the Geneva Conventions Act 1957
l) Mutiny
m) Piracy
n) Soliciting, incitement, attempt or conspiracy to commit any of the above offences

Class 2:

a) Rape
b) Sexual intercourse with a girl under 13
c) Incest with girl under 13
d) Assault by penetration
e) Causing a person to engage in sexual activity, where penetration is involved
f) Rape of a child under 13

g) Assault of a child under 13 by penetration
h) Causing or inciting a child under 13 to engage in sexual activity, where penetration is involved
i) Sexual activity with a person with a mental disorder, where penetration is involved
j) Inducement to procure sexual activity with a mentally disordered person where penetration is involved
k) Paying for sexual services of a child where child is under 13 and penetration is involved
l) Committing an offence with intent to commit a sexual offence, where the offence is kidnapping or false imprisonment;
m) Soliciting, incitement, attempt of conspiracy to commit any of the above.

Class 3:
All other offences not listed in classes 1 or 2.

**Either way offences may be committed by the magistrates' courts to the Crown Court for trial. The magistrates are required to ask defendants to indicate their plea to charge. Where a guilty plea is indicated, the summary trial procedure is deemed to have been complied with and the defendant is deemed to have pleaded guilty under it.

- Where a defendant indicates a not guilty plea or gives no indication on his plea, the court, having had regard to various factors, including representations by the prosecution and the defence, indicates whether it considers the offence more suitable for summary trial than on indictment. However, a court may only proceed to summary trial with the consent of the defendant.

- Since 15 January 2001 all indictable only cases have been 'sent for trial' to the Crown Court after they have had their first appearance in the magistrates' court. This procedure under Section 51 of the Crime and Disorder Act 1998 replaced committal proceedings and reduces the number of hearings these cases have at the magistrates' court. While the time that indictable only cases spend in the Crown Court has increased, it is hoped that the overall time from arrest to sentence will decrease. The Criminal Procedure Rules 2005 introduced new principles of case management for cases sent or committed for trial. On receipt at the Crown Court, such cases have a Plea and Case Management Hearing (PCMH) at which directions may be given for the future conduct of the case including, if appropriate, the fixing of the date for trial or the warned period for its listing. In specific cases, it is possible for the PCMH to be dispensed with in favour of a written procudure.

Committals for Sentence

Provisions in the Magistrates' Courts Act 1980 allow magistrates to commit defendants who have been summarily convicted of an either way offence to the Crown Court for sentence. The magistrates must be of the opinion that the offence or the combination of the offence and one or more offences associated with it is so serious that a greater punishment should be inflicted than they have power to impose or, in the case of a violent or sexual offence, that a sentence of imprisonment for a longer term than they have power to impose is necessary to protect the public from serious harm. Committals may also arise from breaches of the terms of, for example, community rehabilitation orders or of suspended sentences of imprisonment.

Appeals

In its appellate jurisdiction the Crown Court deals mainly with appeals against conviction and/or sentence in respect of criminal offences, including consequential orders such as disqualification from driving, and against the making of certain stand alone orders such as Anti-Social Behaviour Orders. The Crown Court may dismiss or allow the appeal and vary all or any part of the sentence.

Appeal are usually heard by a circuit judge sitting with no more than four lay magistrates (normally two).

Receipts, Disposals and Results

During 2005, 80,021 cases were received for trial at the Crown Court, an increase of 1% on the 2004 total. Committals for trial disposed of during 2005 totalled 77,175, a decrease of nearly 6%. As receipts exceeded disposals the number of cases outstanding increased by just over 10% to 31,063 compared with 28,198 at the end of 2004.

Table 6.1
Committals for trial, committals for sentence, and appeals: Number of cases received and disposed of, 1990 to 2005

	Committals for trial[1]		Committals for sentence		Appeals	
Year	Receipts[2]	Disposal[3]	Receipts[2]	Disposal[3]	Receipts[2]	Disposal[3]
1990	103,011	100,005	15,270	14,988	17,801	17,557
1991	104,754	101,999	16,554	15,995	19,150	18,433
1992	100,994	100,742	14,883	15,546	20,783	19,765
1993	86,849	85,566	11,088	10,956	24,531	23,722
1994	89,301	86,980	11,485	11,226	25,262	25,644
1995	81,186	88,985	11,718	11,726	25,240	26,062
1996	83,328	83,274	12,002	11,762	18,981	20,304
1997	91,110	90,096	14,871	13,378	16,269	16,196
1998	75,815	77,794	29,774	28,224	16,278	16,473
1999	74,232	73,539	31,928	30,641	15,413	15,381
2000	71,002	72,762	27,591	28,713	13,902	14,359
2001	80,551	75,565	25,960	25,717	12,596	12,679
2002	83,449	81,766	28,837	28,235	11,910	11,940
2003	84,412	83,497	30,757	30,328	11,858	11,746
2004	79,232	81,750	31,156	30,979	12,882	12,578
2005	80,021	77,175	32,937	32,348	12,843	12,809

1 Since 2001 figures for committals for trial include cases sent for trial under s51 CDA 1998

2 Receipts include committals direct from PSDs, bench warrants executed (trial and sentence only) and cases transferred in, less cases transferred out

3 Disposals are total cases dealt with

Table 6.2
Committals for trial: Cases received and disposed of and outstanding at end of year, by region, 2005

Region	Receipts[1]	Disposal[2]	Outstanding
London	16,191	15,320	7,038
Midlands	14,361	14,091	5,588
North East	11,762	11,817	3,827
North West	12,474	12,187	4,764
South East	12,852	11,572	5,810
South West	7,127	6,996	2,685
Wales and Cheshire	5,254	5,192	1,351
England & Wales	**80,021**	**77,175**	**31,063**

[1] Receipts include committals direct from PSDs, bench warrants executed (trial and sentence only) and cases transferred in, less cases transferred out

[2] Disposals are total cases dealt with

Tables 6.3 to 6.5 illustrate the distribution of committals for trial disposed of according to class of case. The total number of cases disposed of decreased by 4,575 on the 2004 figure.

Table 6.3
Committals for trial: Number of cases disposed of, showing percentage in each class of case, 2005

Region	Class 1	Class 2	Class 3 & 4	Total disposed
London	2.0	3.2	94.8	15,320
Midlands	1.5	4.8	93.7	14,091
North East	1.3	4.3	94.4	11,817
North West	1.5	3.8	94.7	12,187
South East	1.2	4.8	94.0	11,572
South West	1.5	5.0	93.5	6,996
Wales and Cheshire	1.4	4.2	94.4	5,192
England & Wales	**1.5**	**4.2**	**94.2**	**77,175**

Table 6.4

Committals for trial: Cases involving a not guilty please disposed of showing percentage in each class, 2005

Region	Class 1	Class 2	Class 3 & 4	Total disposed
London	3.5	5.3	91.2	6,972
Midlands	3.1	9.9	87.0	4,130
North East	2.2	9.0	88.9	3,358
North West	2.8	6.9	90.2	4,173
South East	1.5	8.3	90.2	4,446
South West	2.3	8.9	88.9	2,640
Wales and Cheshire	2.2	6.9	90.9	2,160
England & Wales	**2.6**	**7.6**	**89.7**	**27,879**

Table 6.5

Committals for trial: Cases heard[1] by High Court judges as percentage of all cases heard, in each class, 2005

	Class 1		Class 2		Class 3 &4	
Region	Number of cases heard	% heard by High Court judge	Number of cases heard	% heard by High Court judge	Number of cases heard	% heard by High Court judge
London	296	4.1	433	0.5	13,031	0.3
Midlands	199	39.7	606	5.1	11,813	1.6
North East	145	35.9	479	5.8	10,056	1.8
North West	180	45.6	419	4.8	10,261	1.2
South East	135	25.2	519	3.1	9,933	1.2
South West	102	43.1	329	5.5	5,995	1.5
Wales and Cheshire	70	41.4	205	5.4	4,549	1.8
England & Wales	**1,127**	**29.5**	**2,990**	**4.2**	**65,638**	**1.3**

[1] Excludes bench warrants issued, unfit to plead, left on file etc.

Nearly 84% of committals for trial were heard by circuit judges, with recorders accounting for a further over 13%. High Court judges heard nearly 2% of cases and deputy High Court and deputy circuit judges between them dealt with less than 1%.

Table 6.6
Committals for trial: Cases dealt with[1] in each region, by type of judge, 2005

Region	High Court Judge	Deputy High Court Judge	Circuit Judge	Deputy Circuit Judge	Recorder	Total
London	54	4	11,357	186	2,159	13,760
Midlands	302	3	10,454	45	1,814	12,618
North East	261	1	8,769	23	1,626	10,680
North West	228	24	9,566	54	988	10,860
South East	169	6	8,867	183	1,362	10,587
South West	153	2	5,252	51	968	6,426
Wales and Cheshire	120	–	4,189	6	509	4,824
England & Wales	**1,287**	**40**	**58,454**	**548**	**9,426**	**69,755**

[1] Excludes bench warrants issued, unfit to plead, left on file etc.

A ‘cracked’ trial is a case that is listed at the Crown Court for a contested trial by jury but on the day of the trial, for one of a number of reasons, it is disposed of in some other way. The largest percentage of cracked trials occur when the defendant pleads guilty on the trial date (62.5% in 2005).

Other main reasons for cracking include where the prosecution accepts a plea of guilty to an alternative charge (nearly 20%), the prosecution offer no evidence (nearly 17%) and the defendant being bound over in a sum of money to keep the peace for a specified period (over 2%). The percentage of cracked trials as a proportion of all cases disposed of decreased to over 22%.

Table 6.7
Cracked Trials: By reason for crack, 2005

	Defendant pleads guilty		Prosecution accepts guilty plea		No evidence offered		Bind over		Unfit to plead/ deceased		Total
Region	Number	%	Number	%	Number	%	Number	%	Number	%	Number
London	1,377	58.2	309	13.0	620	26.2	54	2.3	8	0.3	2,368
Midlands	1,593	61.6	491	19.0	437	16.9	62	2.4	3	0.1	2,586
North East	2,249	65.2	649	18.8	471	13.7	71	2.1	8	0.2	3,448
North West	1,754	64.2	559	20.5	365	13.4	55	2.0	0	0.0	2,733
South East	1,136	63.0	297	16.5	314	17.4	50	2.8	5	0.3	1,802
South West	586	61.0	181	18.9	162	16.9	27	2.8	4	0.4	960
Wales and Cheshire	437	61.1	173	24.2	89	12.4	15	2.1	1	0.1	715
England & Wales	**9,132**	**62.5**	**2,659**	**18.2**	**2,458**	**16.8**	**334**	**2.3**	**29**	**0.2**	**14,612**

Tables 6.8 to 6.11 show how cases and defendants committed for trial are dealt with, according to plea. A guilty plea is recorded when a defendant –

a) pleads guilty to all counts

b) pleads guilty to some counts and not guilty to others and no jury is sworn in respect of the not guilty counts

c) pleads not guilty to some or all counts but offers a guilty plea to alternatives which are accepted (providing no jury is sworn in respect of other counts)

A case is treated as a guilty plea only if pleas of guilty are recorded in respect of all defendants.

In 2005 the number of not guilty plea cases was over 7% lower than in 2004; also the number of guilty plea cases showed a decrease of over 1%. The guilty plea rate was just under 60% (over 58% in 2004).

Table 6.8
Committals for trial: Cases dealt with[1], according to plea, 2005

Region	Not Guilty	Guilty	% Guilty
London	6,972	6,672	48.9
Midlands	4,130	8,459	67.2
North East	3,358	7,290	68.5
North West	4,173	6,605	61.3
South East	4,446	6,121	57.9
South West	2,640	3,780	58.9
Wales and Cheshire	2,160	2,651	55.1
England & Wales	**27,879**	**41,578**	**59.9**

[1] Excludes cases where no plea was recorded i.e. bench warrants issued, unfit to plead, left on file etc.

During 2005, over 66% of the defendants who pleaded not guilty to all counts were acquitted representing over 17% of the total 89,861 dealt with. Of these, just over 57% were discharged by the judge, over 11% were acquitted on the direction of the judge and over 31% were acquitted by a jury. Of the defendants convicted in 2005 after a plea of not guilty to some or all counts, 21% were convicted on a majority verdict by a jury, the remainder being convicted unanimously.

Table 6.9
Committals for trial: Defendants dealt with showing result according to plea, 2005

		Not guilty to all counts				Not guilty to some counts			All Defendants
Region	Guilty	Acquitted	Convicted	Total	% acquitted	Acquitted	Convicted	Total	Total[1]
London	7,863	4,355	2,290	6,645	65.5%	229	231	460	14,968
Midlands	10,214	2,472	1,140	3,612	68.4%	259	127	386	14,212
North East	8,809	1,913	917	2,830	67.6%	149	115	264	11,903
North West	7,754	2,084	881	2,965	70.3%	548	101	649	11,368
South East	7,220	2,595	1,545	4,140	62.7%	151	167	318	11,678
South West	4,379	1,559	840	2,399	65.0%	160	97	257	7,035
Wales & Cheshire	3,151	938	498	1,436	65.3%	494	83	577	5,164
England & Wales	**49,390**	**15,916**	**8,111**	**24,027**	**66.2%**	**1,990**	**921**	**2,911**	**76,328**

[1] Excludes 13,553 defendants for whom: bench warrant issued, no plea recorded, indictment to lie on file, found unfit to plead, and other results

Table 6.10

Committals for trial: Defendants acquitted[1] after a plea of not guilty showing the number and manner of acquittal, 2005

Region	Not guilty to all counts				Not guilty to some counts			
	Discharged by judge	Acquittal directed by judge	Jury verdict	Total acquittals	Discharged by judge	Acquittal directed by judge	Jury verdict	Total acquittals
London	2,455	566	1,370	4,391	20	63	148	231
Midlands	1,566	241	667	2,474	12	44	204	260
North East	1,204	208	505	1,917	6	42	101	149
North West	1,168	224	702	2,094	27	48	479	554
South East	1,454	298	847	2,599	9	42	103	154
South West	842	186	531	1,559	17	26	117	160
Wales & Cheshire	434	126	383	943	28	24	443	495
England & Wales	**9,123**	**1,849**	**5,005**	**15,977**	**119**	**289**	**1,595**	**2,003**

[1] Acquitted on those counts to which they pleaded not guilty

Table 6.11

Committals for trial: Defendants convicted after a plea of not guilty showing the number and percentage convicted on a majority verdict, and the number of dissenting jurors, 2005

Region	Convicted after plea of not guilty[1]	Majority verdicts			
		Dissentients			
		1	2	Total	as % of convictions
London	2,553	231	384	615	24%
Midlands	1,271	98	148	246	19%
North East	1,038	82	118	200	19%
North West	993	78	117	195	20%
South East	1,713	127	225	352	21%
South West	941	80	146	226	24%
Wales and Cheshire	581	30	68	98	17%
England & Wales	**9,090**	**726**	**1,206**	**1,932**	**21%**

[1] Convicted on at least one count to which the defendant pleaded not guilty

In 2005 the number of committals for sentence received at the Crown Court increased by almost 6% to 32,937, whilst disposals increased by over 4% to 32,348. The number outstanding at the end of 2005 increased by nearly 10% to 4,261.

Table 6.12
Committals for sentence[1]: Cases received and disposed of and outstanding at end of year, by region, 2005

Region	Receipts[2]	Disposals[3]	Outstanding
London	5,638	5,449	744
Midlands	6,237	6,284	738
North East	5,096	5,074	676
North West	4,833	4,686	693
South East	5,239	5,057	707
South West	3,671	3,659	461
Wales and Cheshire	2,223	2,139	242
England & Wales	**32,937**	**32,348**	**4,261**

[1] Includes committals from PSDs after breach, bring backs and deferred sentences

[2] Receipts include committals direct from PSDs, bench warrants executed (trial and sentence only) and cases transferred in, less cases transferred out

[3] Disposals are total cases dealt with

Appeals received in 2005 decreased by less than 1% compared with 2004 (12,843 and 12,882 respectively) whilst disposals increased by almost 2% (to 12,809 from 12,578). The number of appeals outstanding decreased by 0.4% to 2,071.

Of the appellants dealt with in 2005, 5,537 (just over 43%) had their appeals allowed or their sentence varied. Of the remainder, 3,791 (nearly 30%) were dismissed and 3,477 (27%) were abandoned or otherwise disposed.

Table 6.13
Appeals against decisions of magistrates' courts: Appeals received and disposed of and outstanding at end of year, by region, 2005

Region	Receipts[1]	Disposals[2]	Outstanding
London	1,817	1,826	373
Midlands	2,219	2,186	330
North East	1,997	1,964	295
North West	1,869	1,876	312
South East	2,508	2,528	430
South West	1,470	1,470	221
Wales and Cheshire	963	959	110
England & Wales	**12,843**	**12,809**	**2,071**

[1] Receipts include committals direct from PSDs, bench warrants executed (trial and sentence only) and cases transferred in, less cases transferred out

[2] Disposals are total cases dealt with

Table 6.14
Appeals against decisions of magistrates' courts: Appellants dealt with showing results, 2005

Region	Allowed	Dismissed	Varied	Abandoned[1] or otherwise disposed[2]	Total
London	595	579	199	453	1,826
Midlands	560	558	428	639	2,185
North East	681	545	194	544	1,964
North West	448	559	354	515	1,876
South East	702	811	305	708	2,526
South West	411	428	238	392	1,469
Wales and Cheshire	254	311	168	226	959
England & Wales	**3,651**	**3,791**	**1,886**	**3,477**	**12,805**

[1] Includes both abandoned in court and abandoned before court appearance

[2] includes those remitted to the magistrates' court

Waiting Times

Details of waiting times are given in Tables 6.15 to 6.20. They show the waiting times between committal or lodging of an appeal, and start of Crown Court hearing for defendants and appellants whose cases were heard during 2005.

Table 6.15
Committals for trial: Defendants dealt with[1] showing average waiting time (weeks) and percentages who waited less than 8 weeks and less than 16 weeks, 2005

			% waiting less than	
Region	No. of defendants	Average waiting time	8 weeks	16 weeks
London	14,968	17.6	31.7%	56.5%
Midlands	14,212	15.3	37.1%	65.3%
North East	11,903	13.0	39.4%	72.4%
North West	11,368	14.6	36.5%	65.9%
South East	11,678	17.5	32.8%	59.3%
South West	7,035	15.3	35.2%	65.8%
Wales and Cheshire	5,164	10.5	50.2%	81.9%
England & Wales	**76,328**	**15.3**	**36.4%**	**65.1%**

[1] Includes bench warrants issued, no plea recorded, indictment to lie on file and found unfit to plead

Waiting times of defendants tend to vary according to the plea entered and whether the defendant is on bail or in custody. On average, defendants who pleaded guilty during 2005 waited 12 weeks whilst those who pleaded not guilty waited 21 weeks. Defendants committed on bail waited an average of 16 weeks in 2005 and for those committed in custody the average was 14 weeks. Waiting times also vary by region; in 2005 the shortest average waiting time was in the Wales and Cheshire region – nearly 11 weeks – while the longest was nearly 18 weeks in the South East region.

Table 6.16

Committals for trial: Defendants dealt with[1] showing percentages who waited less than 8 weeks and less than 16 weeks according to plea, 2005

	Defendants pleading guilty			Defendants pleading not guilty		
		% waiting less than			% waiting less than	
Region	Number	8 weeks	16 weeks	Number	8 weeks	16 weeks
London	7,863	45.4%	72.0%	7,105	14.2%	37.5%
Midlands	10,214	45.1%	74.4%	3,998	14.1%	39.5%
North East	8,809	46.9%	79.0%	3,094	16.2%	53.8%
North West	7,754	47.7%	76.3%	3,614	14.2%	44.9%
South East	7,220	44.6%	72.8%	4,458	10.4%	34.2%
South West	4,379	45.7%	76.5%	2,656	13.1%	45.3%
Wales and Cheshire	3,151	61.4%	88.4%	2,013	28.0%	70.3%
England & Wales	**49,390**	**46.9%**	**76.0%**	**26,938**	**14.7%**	**43.3%**

[1] Includes bench warrants issued, no plea recorded, indictment to lie on file and found unfit to plead

Table 6.17

Committals for trial: Defendants dealt with[1] showing percentages who waited less than 8 weeks and less than 16 weeks according to whether on bail or in custody, 2005

	Defendants on bail			Defendants in custody		
		% waiting less than			% waiting less than	
Region	Number	8 weeks	16 weeks	Number	8 weeks	16 weeks
London	9,114	29.9%	51.5%	5,854	31.7%	62.0%
Midlands	9,786	35.9%	62.4%	4,426	37.4%	69.3%
North East	8,358	37.9%	71.2%	3,545	41.3%	75.4%
North West	8,101	36.5%	64.0%	3,267	38.5%	72.0%
South East	8,063	30.3%	54.4%	3,615	34.4%	66.1%
South West	4,994	31.8%	63.2%	2,041	37.3%	68.5%
Wales and Cheshire	3,685	47.5%	81.2%	1,479	50.4%	81.9%
England & Wales	**52,101**	**34.8%**	**62.3%**	**24,227**	**37.1%**	**69.0%**

[1] Includes bench warrants issued, no plea recorded, indictment to lie on file and found unfit to plead

Table 6.18

Committals for trial: Average waiting time of defendants dealt with[1] whether pleading guilty or not guilty and whether committed on bail or in custody, 2004

Region	Defendants pleading guilty	Defendants pleading not guilty	Defendants on bail	Defendants in custody
London	12.9	22.8	18.5	16.2
Midlands	12.6	22.4	16.0	14.0
North East	11.0	18.4	13.4	11.8
North West	11.8	20.7	15.3	12.9
South East	13.2	24.4	18.6	14.9
South West	12.0	20.7	15.7	14.2
Wales and Cheshire	8.3	13.8	10.4	10.6
England & Wales	**12.0**	**21.3**	**15.9**	**14.0**

[1] Includes bench warrants issued, no plea recorded, indictment to lie on file and found unfit to plead

Table 6.19

Committals for sentence[1]: Defendants dealt with, showing average waiting time (weeks) and percentages who waited less than 8 weeks and less than 16 weeks, 2005

			% waiting less than	
Region	No. of defendants	Average waiting time	8 weeks	16 weeks
London	5,437	5.6	87.0%	97.5%
Midlands	6,249	5.9	83.4%	95.1%
North East	5,067	6.0	81.8%	95.7%
North West	4,653	6.0	82.2%	95.3%
South East	5,077	6.9	75.0%	94.5%
South West	3,663	6.0	81.0%	95.3%
Wales and Cheshire	2,144	3.9	93.2%	98.5%
England & Wales	**32,290**	**5.9**	**82.7%**	**95.8%**

[1] Excludes committals after breach, 'bring backs' and deferred sentence

Table 6.20
Appeals against decisions of magistrates' courts: Appellants dealt with[1], showing average waiting time (weeks) and percentages who waited less than 8 weeks and less than 16 weeks, 2005

Region	No. of appellants	Average waiting time	% waiting less than 8 weeks	% waiting less than 16 weeks
London	1,491	8.2	59.6%	88.3%
Midlands	1,839	7.1	69.7%	90.9%
North East	1,659	5.9	75.1%	95.2%
North West	1,596	6.3	75.9%	95.1%
South East	2,010	9.5	57.9%	84.1%
South West	1,197	7.3	67.0%	93.1%
Wales and Cheshire	807	6.3	73.4%	94.9%
England & Wales	**10,599**	**7.4**	**67.8%**	**91.1%**

[1] Excludes case abandoned before appearance in court

Other Waiting Times Statistics

Information concerning waiting times for cases involving persistent young offenders in the Crown Court is collected by the Department for Constitutional Affairs and is a National Statistic. During 2005 the average time between arrest and sentence for persistent young offenders sentenced in the Crown Court was 186 days.

Hearing Times

Table 6.21
Average hearing times[1] (hours) for cases disposed of, 2005

Region	Committal for trial: Not guilty pleas: Total cases	Committal for trial: Not guilty pleas: average hearing time	Committal for trial: Guilty pleas: Total cases	Committal for trial: Guilty pleas: average hearing time	Cases for sentence[2]: Total cases	Cases for sentence[2]: average hearing time	Appeals[3]: Total cases	Appeals[3]: average hearing time
London	6,972	13.1	6,672	1.7	4,665	0.8	1,463	1.5
Midlands	4,130	8.8	8,459	1.1	5,502	0.5	1,808	0.9
North East	3,358	6.6	7,290	1.0	4,437	0.5	1,632	0.8
North West	4,173	7.4	6,605	1.2	3,887	0.6	1,576	1.1
South East	4,446	10.6	6,121	1.5	4,505	0.7	1,987	1.3
South West	2,640	10.7	3,780	1.2	3,086	0.6	1,179	1.0
Wales and Cheshire	2,160	7.7	2,651	1.3	1,891	0.5	803	1.0
England & Wales	**27,879**	**9.8**	**41,578**	**1.3**	**27,973**	**0.6**	**10,448**	**1.1**

[1] Hearing times exclude lunch adjournments

[2] Includes cases brought back or deferred for sentence but excludes those with no hearing

[3] Excludes cases abandoned before appearance in court

The Magistrates Court

Introduction

This chapter refers to Criminal Proceedings in the Magistrates Courts Information on family proceedings can be found at chapter 5.

All criminal cases start in the Magistrates' Court and 95% are completed there. Magistrates' Courts deal with all ancillary matters connected to criminal cases and also deal with civil cases e.g. family matters, betting and gaming.

A panel of three magistrates supported by a legally qualified Court Clerk usually hears cases in the Magistrates' Courts. A District Judge hears the more complex or sensitive cases. There are approximately 30,000 Magistrates and 130 District Judges in the Magistrates Courts of England & Wales.

Magistrates cannot normally order sentences of imprisonment that exceed 6 months (or 12 months for consecutive sentences) or fines exceeding £5,000. In triable-either way cases or indictable cases the offender may be committed by the magistrates to the Crown Court for sentencing if a more severe sentence is thought to be appropriate.

Effective Ineffective & Cracked Trials

Magistrates Courts record the number and outcome of trials. Uncontested summary matters are not recorded. Trial outcomes are listed as 'Effective', 'Ineffective' or 'Cracked'. Efficient case progression and good inter-agency communication will lead to higher numbers of effective trials and lower numbers of ineffective and cracked trials. Ineffective and cracked trials create additional costs to the justice system and cause inconvenience and delay to witnesses and other court users, therefore this is an important measure for court management.

Table 7.1
Ineffective Trials

	2003		2004		2005	
Region	Number	%	Number	%	Number	%
London	11,073	37.6%	12,815	33.6%	8,862	25.7%
Midlands	11,559	28.7%	10,923	25.6%	8,754	22.8%
North East	6,509	28.7%	6,360	25.2%	5,145	21.3%
North West	6,877	27.6%	6,459	23.8%	5,288	19.8%
South East	7,750	27.6%	7,091	24.1%	6,229	20.6%
South West	4,773	27.6%	4,007	23.3%	3,107	20.0%
Wales & Cheshire	3,675	24.4%	2,731	19.6%	2,249	17.1%
England & Wales	**52,216**	**29.4%**	**50,386**	**26.0%**	**39,634**	**21.7%**

Definition of Ineffective Trial – The trial is adjourned due to action or inaction by one or more of the parties.

National performance targets have been set for ineffective trials in each financial year as follows: 2003/4 – 26.5%, 2004/5 – 24.5%, 2005/6 – 23% with a targeted reduction to 19% by 2008. Each Magistrates Court Area has its own target set at the start of the financial year to enable the national target to be achieved. The target is measured in the final quarter of the financial year.

In the final quarter of the 2004/5 financial year the national ineffective rate was 22.7%, outperforming the target by 1.8%.

The main reason given for a trial becoming ineffective in 2005 was 'prosecution witness absent (other)' (4.0%) other main reasons are 'defendant absent, did not attend' and 'defence not ready'.

Table 7.2
Cracked Trials

	2003			2004			2005		
	Result*	Non-result**	Total Cracked	Result*	Non-result**	Total Cracked	Result*	Non-result**	Total Cracked
London	17.6%	13.9%	31.5%	18.0%	14.0%	31.9%	19.4%	14.7%	34.1%
Midlands	25.2%	16.1%	41.3%	25.1%	14.7%	39.7%	25.0%	13.8%	38.8%
North East	26.1%	13.5%	39.6%	25.4%	13.1%	38.6%	24.9%	12.2%	37.2%
North West	25.4%	16.2%	41.6%	25.9%	17.3%	43.2%	26.3%	15.6%	41.9%
South East	22.3%	13.2%	35.5%	21.8%	13.0%	34.8%	22.3%	12.0%	34.3%
South West	19.4%	14.1%	33.5%	19.6%	12.9%	32.6%	19.9%	12.2%	32.1%
Wales & Cheshire	26.6%	14.3%	40.9%	27.1%	13.7%	40.8%	25.9%	12.6%	38.5%
England & Wales	**23.2%**	**14.6%**	**37.8%**	**23.0%**	**14.2%**	**37.2%**	**23.3%**	**13.5%**	**36.8%**

Definition of a Cracked Trial – The trial does not go ahead due to either: 1. The defendant pleads guilty or accepts a bind over, or 2. The prosecution ends the case. In either instance, resources are wasted and witnesses are called unnecessarily.

There are no targets for cracked trials

The largest proportion of cracked trials in 2005 occurred due to a late guilty plea (first time offered by the defendant) (17.6%)

Other main reasons for cracking in 2005 included 'prosecution end case, insufficient evidence' and 'prosecution end case, witness withdrawn'.

Timeliness

The Timeliness return measures the number of days taken from the defendant's first court listing to completion of the case in the magistrates' courts. This measure provides information on case progression issues in each court and region; the published measure is untargeted.

Timeliness is measured by surveys structured around Indictable and Triable either way cases and all Criminal Cases.

Table 7.3

Average number of days from first court listing to completion for defendants in Indictable/triable-either-way cases in Magistrates' Courts – 2001-2005[1]

	2001		2002		2003		2004		2005	
Region	sample size	days	sample size	days	sample size	days	sample size	days	sample size	days
London	4,314	53	4,586	52	4,743	56	4,247	56	4,302	53
Midlands	6,445	61	6,660	57	7,022	59	5,705	57	5,451	56
North East & Yorkshire	5,706	56	6,004	55	5,513	58	4,637	55	4,880	55
North West	4,297	55	4,875	59	4,845	61	4,080	58	3,944	56
South East	4,349	50	4,769	53	5,202	52	4,507	55	4,397	56
South West	2,956	53	2,850	47	3,055	47	2,694	44	2,843	47
Wales and Cheshire	2,274	53	2,741	52	2,704	50	2,623	50	2,310	45
England and Wales	**30,341**	**55**	**32,485**	**54**	**33,084**	**56**	**28,493**	**55**	**28,127**	**54**

[1] Results for Indictable/triable-either-way cases based on proceedings in one sample week in March, June, September and December.

Source: DCA Time Intervals Survey

Table 7.4
Average number of days from first court listing to completion for defendants in All Criminal cases in Magistrates' Courts – 2001-2005[1]

	2001		2002		2003		2004		2005	
Region	sample size	days	sample size	days	sample size	days	sample size	days	sample size	days
London	8,199	30	8,361	32	8,633	31	8,730	34	9,240	33
Midlands	11,536	39	11,747	34	12,758	36	13,071	35	11,894	35
North East & Yorkshire	10,144	34	10,510	33	10,738	33	10,417	32	10,509	30
North West	9,016	32	9,843	35	9,992	35	8,973	37	8,615	33
South East	9,618	30	10,546	34	11,446	34	11,241	33	10,553	31
South West	6,117	33	6,574	35	7,207	30	6,479	31	6,861	29
Wales and Cheshire	3,874	34	5,427	27	6,061	25	6,667	25	5,481	24
England and Wales	**58,504**	**33**	**63,008**	**33**	**66,835**	**32**	**65,578**	**33**	**63,153**	**31**

[1] Results for all criminal cases based on proceedings in one sample week in March and September.

Source: DCA Time Intervals Survey

Persistent Young Offenders (Timeliness)

The category of persistent young offender was defined in the Inter-Departmental circular Tackling delays in the Youth Justice System issued on 15 October 1997:

"A persistent young offender is a young person aged 10-17 who has been sentenced by any criminal court in the UK on three or more separate occasions for one or more recordable offence, and within three years of the last sentencing occasion and is subsequently arrested or has an information laid against them for a further recordable offence".

The calculation of the target figure of 71 days, and performance against that target, uses data from the Police National Computer and police forces. The data covers those individuals who fell within the definition of persistent young offender at the date of arrest, and also those who were brought within the definition by further convictions before the time of sentence.

Table 7.5
Annual PYO Arrest to Sentence Times (days)

Overall:	2001	2002	2003	2004	2005*
London	100	84	77	85	86
Midlands	80	67	61	71	71
North East	68	64	71	70	60
North West	77	72	71	73	74
South East	80	67	63	64	62
South West	70	68	62	59	64
Wales and Cheshire	65	61	55	58	63
England and Wales	76	68	66	69	68
PYOs dealt with in the Magistrates' Courts:					
London	91	73	65	73	74
Midlands	71	60	53	62	63
North East	59	58	63	63	55
North West	66	62	61	65	66
South East	72	58	55	56	56
South West	66	62	56	54	59
Wales and Cheshire	62	56	51	54	60
England and Wales	**68**	**61**	**58**	**61**	**60**

* 2005 figures are subject to revision, as the results of the 2005 Arrest to Charge survey have not yet been finalised.

Enforcement

Fines

Fine enforcement is a key area for performance improvement in magistrates' courts and a wide ranging programme of change is being taken forward by Her Majesty's Courts Service (HMCS).

In a concerted effort to increase public confidence and compliance in the first instance, HMCS is rolling out a new statutory framework for fine enforcement in the Courts Act 2003 (including compulsory attachment of earnings orders for defaulters and new sanctions for those who default on fines) and introducing a number of other initiatives aimed at increasing information sharing between departments to aid the tracing of offenders. Longer-term business redesign work is also underway to improve ways of working and further optimise performance.

Performance

The tough new fine enforcement regime introduced to crack down on fine defaulters has ensured that the fines payment rate for the 2004/05 financial year has hit 80% – exceeding its target of 78%. The national fines collection target for the 2005/06 financial year has been set at 81%.

Table 7.6
Payment Rate

	2001	2002	2003	2004	2005
London	47%	38%	52%	64%	62%
Midlands	59%	62%	57%	70%	88%
North East	72%	61%	54%	78%	85%
North West	58%	56%	54%	70%	78%
South East	66%	64%	64%	76%	88%
South West	63%	73%	61%	76%	86%
Wales & Cheshire	54%	57%	55%	88%	96%
England & Wales	**59%**	**56%**	**57%**	**73%**	**82%**

The Payment rate changed in 2003-4 and therefore direct comparisons should not be made between the years, the payment rate calculations are as follows;

Payment Rate Calculation
Payment Rate = *Amount Paid* divided by *New Net Amount Owed*

The primary performance indicator is the payment rate. It is defined as the amount paid into court as a percentage of the new net amount owed. Methods of calculating the new net amounts owed have changed over the last five years and are detailed below:

September 1999 to March 2003 – New Net Amount Owed *includes* Legally Cancelled amounts, Civil monies and Confiscation Orders

April 2003 to December 2003 – New Net Amount Owed *excludes* Legally Cancelled amounts, Civil monies and Confiscation Orders

January 2004 to July 2004 – New Net Amount Owed *excludes* Legally Cancelled amounts, Administratively Cancelled amounts, Civil monies and Confiscation Orders

July 2004 onwards – New Net Amount Owed *excludes* Legally Cancelled amounts, Administratively Cancelled amounts, Civil monies and Confiscation Orders, but *includes* Amounts Written Back

From April 2003 onwards, confiscation and civil amounts have not been included in any of the enforcement calculations. It is not possible to separate those elements out from the figures before that date. As a result of these revisions, direct year-on-year comparisons cannot be made.

Community Penalties

Adults and Youths who breach community penalties become the subject of a community penalty breach warrant. It is important that these breach proceedings are enforced quickly in order to preserve the validity of community penalties as an alternative to fines and custodial sentences.

The Community Penalty Enforcement Group (CPEG) has a wide delivery plan in place to secure improvements in Community Penalty Breach Warrant performance. CPEG is chaired by the National Probation Directorate and is working with HMCS, Probation, Youth Justice Board, Police, the Office for Criminal Justice Reform (OCJR) and through the LCJBs to focus on warrant backlogs, adjournments, quality of information exchange and prioritising warrants. Areas with the poorest performance in respect of breach warrant enforcement are being provided with targeted support and new initiatives (including a case tracker and a fast track process aimed at high-risk offenders) to secure performance improvement.

Table 7.7
% Executed or Withdrawn within Target

	2001-02	2002-03	2003-04	2004-05
London	14%	18%	21%	43%
South East	22%	27%	30%	45%
South West	2%	31%	35%	41%
Wales & Cheshire	15%	20%	56%	58%
North West	27%	31%	39%	46%
Midlands	19%	25%	34%	38%
North East	30%	38%	43%	47%
England & Wales	**24%**	**29%**	**37%**	**45%**

New targets were set in October 2005 for community penalty breach proceedings. Proceedings should take an average of 35 working days from breach to resolution of the case and 50% of all breach proceedings to be resolved within 25 days of breach. These underpin the existing key performance indicator to execute 75% of CPBWs within 20 working days for adults (10 working days for youths).

Department for Constitutional Affairs Tribunals Group

During 2004 DCA had administrative responsibility for –

- Adjudicator to HM Land Registry
- Finance & Tax Tribunals (includes the Special Commissioners of Income Tax, Value Added Tax and Duties Tribunals, Financial Services and Markets Tribunals)
- Gender Recognition Panel (administrative support established end of 2004)
- Immigration Appellate Authority (includes the Immigration Adjudicators and the Immigration Appeals Tribunal (IAT). In April 2005 The Asylum and Immigration Tribunal replaces the Immigration Appellate Authority.)
- Immigration Services Tribunal
- Information Tribunal (administrative support established end of 2004)
- Lands Tribunal
- Pathogen Access Appeals Commission
- Pensions Appeal Tribunals
- Proscribed Organisation Appeals Commission
- Social Security & Child Support Commissioners (now the Commissioners Office)
- Special Immigration Appeals Commission
- Transport Tribunal
- **The Adjudicator to HM Land Registry**

The Adjudicator currently deals with the following –

- Disputed applications to the Land Registry which have not been disposed of by agreement. HM Land Registry must refer such cases to the Adjudicator.
- Applications for putting a document right or setting it aside.

In the future the Adjudicator will also determine appeals against decisions of HM Land Registry concerning Network Access Agreements.

The offices and permanent hearing rooms are in London, but hearings can be arranged anywhere in England and Wales if necessary. Appeal lies to the High Court.

Tribunals: Cases received, 2004

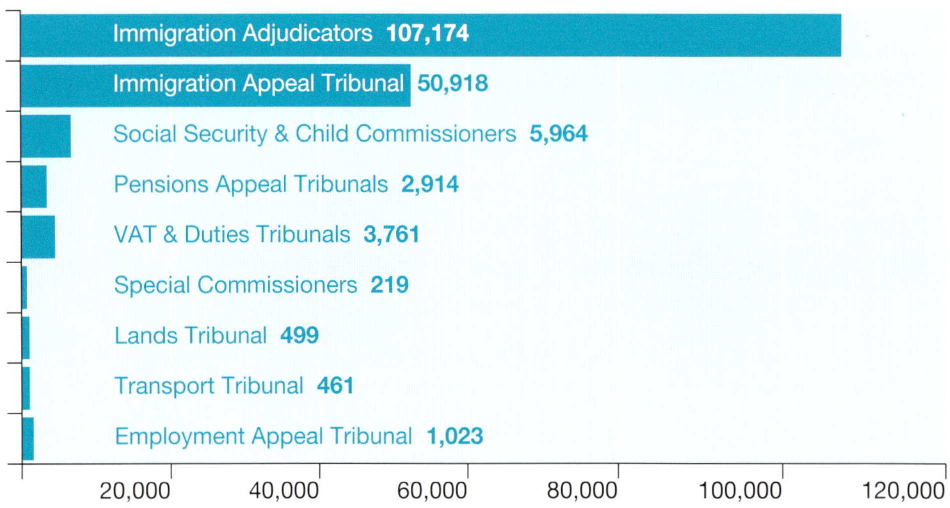

The general enquiries number is 020 7029 9860.

Note: The Adjudicator to HM Land Registry is an independent statutory judicial office holder appointed by the Lord Chancellor under the provisions of the Land Registration Act 2002. His status is not that of a Tribunal established under the Tribunals and Inquiries Act 1992 although he is subject to the supervision of the Council on Tribunals.

Table 8.1
The Adjudicator to HM Land Registry: Referrals and Rectifications received and disposed of in England and Wales, 2005

	Number of cases received	Number of cases disposed of
Referrals:	1,804	1,874
Rectifications:	20	31
Total	**1,824**	**1,905**

The Commissioners' Office (formerly the Office of the Social Security and Child Support Commissioners)
Commissioners are appointed by the Queen to determine applications for leave to appeal and appeals on points of law against decisions made by the Appeal Service (tAS) in Social Security, Tax Credit, Child Support, Housing Benefit, Council Tax Benefit and Compensation Recovery cases. Commissioners also have first-tier jurisdiction in Forfeiture Act cases. During 2005, Commissioners gained additional jurisdiction to deal with appeals in Child Trust Fund cases and appeals from decisions of the Pensions Appeal Tribunals where they sit as Pension Appeal Commissioners.

As at the 31st of December 2005, apart from the Chief Commissioner, there were 17 full-time Commissioners whose jurisdiction cover England, Wales and Scotland. Commissioners decide most appeals on the papers, but may grant an oral hearing requested by a party or may direct one. Hearings are held in London, Cardiff and Edinburgh, and at other centres in major cities in the UK. They also offer oral hearings by video conferencing.

Travelling and subsistence allowances are reimbursed to parties who attend oral hearings.

There are no fees for bringing proceedings and no legal costs are awarded.

Appeals against decisions of the Commissioners lie to the Court of Appeal on a point of law in England and Wales and to the Court of Session in Scotland. Leave to appeal must be obtained from the Commissioner or the Court.

The Tribunal's general enquiries number is 020 7029 9850 and the website address is: www.osscsc.gov.uk

Finance and Tax Tribunals

The Finance and Tax Tribunals are responsible for the administration of four separate tribunals which each have different jurisdictions and rules of procedure.

The Tribunals' general enquiries number is 020 7612 9700 and the website address is: www.financeandtaxtribunals.gov.uk

The VAT and Duties Tribunals
The VAT and Duties Tribunals deal with appeals brought by traders and organisations against decisions made by HM Revenue and Customs (formerly Customs and Excise) which relate to Value Added Tax (VAT), customs duties, excise duties, landfill tax, insurance premium tax and aggregates and climate change levy.

The Tribunals are headed by a President and as at the 31st December 2005 there were five salaried legal Chairmen, and a part-time Vice-President for Scotland. There are also separate panels of fee-paid legally qualified Chairmen for England and Wales, Scotland and Northern Ireland and likewise separate panels of non-legal Members. Many of the Chairmen also sit as Special Commissioners.

There are permanent hearing centres based in Manchester, London and Edinburgh but hearings are also held at other locations across the country including Northern Ireland.

Hearings are informal and appellants are able to present their own appeal or to instruct legal representatives. Each tribunal hearing consists of a legally qualified chairman who on occasion may be accompanied by one or two lay members. A Tribunal has power to award costs.

Appeals against decisions of the VAT and Duties Tribunals may be made on a point of law to the High Court (Chancery Division) or the equivalent authority in Scotland (the Court of Session) and Northern Ireland (the Court of Appeal). Exceptionally, an appeal can be made direct to the Court of Appeal if certain conditions are met.

Table 8.2
The VAT & Duties Tribunals: Appeals received and disposed of, 2005

		Cases disposed of		
	Number of cases received	Heard or determined	Otherwise disposed of	Total
VAT Appeals:	2,312	496	1,751	2,247
Customes & Excise Duties, Insurance Premium Tax, Landfill Tax, Climate Change Levy, Aggregates Levy:	384	112	346	458
Total	**2,696**	**608**	**2,097**	**2,705**

The Special Commissioners

The Special Commissioners hear and determine appeals resulting from decisions of HM Revenue and Customs (formerly the Inland Revenue) relating to all direct taxes including income tax, corporation tax, capital gains tax and inheritance tax. The jurisdiction of the Special Commissioners extends to the whole of the United Kingdom, with appeals heard at four main locations – London, Manchester, Belfast and Edinburgh – but hearings may also be held at other convenient centres throughout the United Kingdom should a more local venue be deemed necessary.

The Tribunal consists of a Presiding Special Commissioner and as at the 31st December 2005 there were five full-time Special Commissioners. There are also 12 deputy Special Commissioners. All also sit as Chairmen of the VAT and Duties Tribunals.

The hearings are informal and appellants are able to present their own appeal or to instruct legal representatives. The Special Commissioners are legally qualified and usually sit alone although two commissioners may sit together for lengthier, complex appeals.

Appeals against decisions of the Special Commissioners may be made on a point of law to the High Court (Chancery Division) or the equivalent authority in Scotland (the Court of Session) and Northern Ireland (the Court of Appeal). Exceptionally, an appeal can be made direct to the Court of Appeal if certain conditions are met.

Table 8.3
The Special Commissioners of Income Tax: Cases received and disposed of, 2005

	Cases disposed of		
Number of cases received	Heard or determined	Otherwise disposed of	Total
446	105	113	218

The Financial Services and Markets Tribunal

The Financial Services and Markets Tribunal is an independent judicial body established under Section 132 of the Financial Services and Markets Act 2000 and hears references arising from decision notices which are issued by the Financial Services Authority (FSA). The decision notices issued by the FSA cover a wide range of regulatory and disciplinary matters and the organisation or individual to whom the notices are directed have the right to refer the matter to the Tribunal. The Tribunal will determine the appropriate course of action for the FSA to take.

The majority of hearings are heard in London although the Tribunal will sit at other locations within the UK where appropriate. Each Tribunal hearing consists of a legally qualified chairman and may include one or two lay members with specialist experience within the financial sector.

Appeals against decisions of the Financial Services and Markets Tribunal are made directly to the Court of Appeal.

Table 8.4
Financial Services and Markets Tribunal: Cases received and disposed of, 2005

Number of cases received	Cases disposed of: Heard or determined	Cases disposed of: Otherwise disposed of	Cases disposed of: Total
31	19	26	45

The Pensions Regulator Tribunal – from April 2005

The Pensions Regulator Tribunal is an independent judicial body established in April 2005 under section 102 of the Pensions Act 2004. The Tribunal hears references arising from certain decisions issued by the Pensions Regulator. The firm or the individual to whom the decision notice is directed has the right to refer the matter to the Tribunal which will determine the appropriate action for the Pensions Regulator to take.

The majority of hearings will be heard in London although the Tribunal will sit at other locations within the UK where appropriate. Each Tribunal hearing consists of a legally qualified chairman and may include one or two lay members with special experience of the financial regulatory environment or the operation of pension schemes. Appeals against decisions of the Pensions Regulator Tribunal are made directly to the Court of Appeal.

Table 8.5
Pensions Regulator Tribunal: Cases received and disposed of, 2005

Number of cases received	Cases disposed of: Heard or determined	Cases disposed of: Otherwise disposed of	Cases disposed of: Total
1	0	0	0

Gender Recognition Panel

The Gender Recognition Panel was established by the Gender Recognition Act 2004. This allows individuals to be granted legal recognition of their acquired gender.

The President of the Gender Recognition Panel is also President of the Appeals Service (tAS). He is supported by a Deputy President, 6 legally qualified members and 6 medical members who are also members of The Appeal Service (tAS).

Cases are mainly decided on paper applications to the panel.

Table 8.6
Gender Recognition Panel, cases received and disposed, 2005

Number of cases received	Cases disposed of		
	Heard or determined	Otherwise disposed of	Total
1,242	1,011	16	1,027

The general enquiries number is 0845 3555155.

Asylum & Immigration Tribunal (AIT)

On 4th April 2005 the commencement of section 26 of *The Asylum and Immigration (Treatment of Claimants, etc.) Act 2004* introduced a unified asylum and immigration appeals system under the newly established Asylum and Immigration Tribunal AIT). The AIT was created by a merger of the Immigration Adjudicators and the Immigration Appeals Tribunal (IAT).

The purpose of the Tribunal is to hear and decide appeals against decisions made by the Home Office, and entry clearance officers, to –

- Refuse a person political asylum in the UK;
- Refuse a person entry to, or leave to remain, in the UK for permanent settlement;
- Deport someone already in the UK to their country of origin;
- Refuse a person entry to the UK for a family visit.

One of the key differences between the AIT and the previous two tier structure is the direct lodgement of appeals to the Tribunal. Prior to the 4th April 2005, appeals were lodged with the original decision maker (dependent on whether the appellant was in the UK or overseas).

As at 31st December 2005 the senior judicial structure of the Tribunal consists of the President, Mr Justice Hodge, Deputy Presidents Mr C.M.G Ockelton and Ms E. Arfon-Jones, with Resident Senior Immigration Judges at each AIT hearing centre throughout the UK. There are 385 fee paid Immigration Judges, 185 salaried Immigration Judges and 60 Non-Legal Members.

The jurisdiction of the Tribunal covers the whole of the United Kingdom with 9 main hearing centres including Taylor House in Central London, Hatton Cross, Birmingham, Bradford, Manchester, Stoke, Newport, North Shields and Glasgow.

The Tribunal's general enquiries number is 0845 6000 877 and the website address is: www.ait.gov.uk

Table 8.7
The Immigration Adjudicators: Appeals received and disposed of, January to March 2005

	Asylum	Immigration	Visit Visa	Total
Receipts	8,079	8,720	6,024	**22,823**
Disposed of	11,083	6,215	3,784	**21,082**

Table 8.8
The Immigration Appeals Tribunal: Cases received and disposed of, January to March 2005

	Applications			Appeals			
	Asylum	Immigration	Visit Visa	Asylum	Immigration	Visit Visa	Total
Receipts	6,181	979	736	2,100	497	127	**10,620**
Disposed of	8,877	1,923	803	3,472	481	197	**15,753**

Table 8.9
The Asylum and Immigration Tribunal: Cases received and disposed of, 4th April to December 2005*

	Asylum	Immigration	Visit Visa	Total
Receipts	16,812	62,023	49,738	**128,573**
Disposed of	22,859	34,002	18,077	**74,938**

* The AIT was formed on 4th April 2005 and replaced the IAA. Data for April 2005 excludes IAA cases for 1 April 2005.

Table 8.10
The Asylum and Immigration Tribunal: Cases where reconsideration ordered and disposals, 4th April to December 2005*

	Reconsiderations			
	Asylum	Immigration	Visit Visa	Total
Receipts	3,738	1,562	524	**5,824**
Disposed of	3,582	700	314	**4,596**

* The AIT was formed on 4th April 2005 and replaced the IAA. Data for April 2005 excludes IAA cases for 1 April 2005.

The Special Immigration Appeals Commission (SIAC)

The Special Immigration Appeals Commission is an independent commission established by the Special Immigration Appeals Commission Act 1997. The current Chairman of the Special Immigration Appeals Commission is Mr Justice Ouseley.

The Secretary of State for Constitutional Affairs is responsible for appointing members of the Commission. Jurisdiction covers the whole of the United Kingdom with dedicated hearing facilities in central London.

Table 8.11
The Immigration Services Tribunal: Appeals and applications received and disposed of, 2005

		Cases disposed of		
	Number of cases received	Heard or determined	Otherwise disposed of	Total disposed of
Appeals:				
against decision of OISC	10	10	9	19
Applications:				
Disciplinary charges	2	1	0	1
Total	**12**	**11**	**9**	**20**

The Proscribed Organisation Appeals Commission (POAC)

The Proscribed Organisation Appeals Commission is an independent tribunal established by the Terrorism Act 2000. It deals with cases where the Secretary of State for the Home Department (or, in the case of organisations concerned in terrorism connected with the affairs of Northern Ireland, the Secretary of State for Northern Ireland) refuses an application to remove an organisation from the list of proscribed organisations under the Terrorism Act 2000.

The Secretary of State for Constitutional Affairs is responsible for appointing members of the Commission. Jurisdiction covers the whole of the United Kingdom with a dedicated hearing centre based in central London. The current Chairman of the Proscribed Organisation Appeals Commission is Lord Justice Mantell.

The Pathogens Access Appeals Commission

The Commission hears appeals against decisions to restrict a person's access to a prescribed set of dangerous pathogens and toxins and regarding the arrangements for keeping such materials. It was established under the provisions of the Anti-Terrorism Crime and Security Act 2001. The current Chairman of the Pathogens Access Appeals Commission is Lord Justice Mantell.

Immigration Services Tribunal

The Immigration Services Tribunal was created by the Immigration, Nationality and Asylum Act 1999. It is not connected to the Asylum and Immigration Tribunal and has the following functions –

- to hear appeals against decisions of the Office of the Immigration Services Commissioner concerning the registration of immigration advisors, and
- to consider disciplinary charges brought by the Commissioner against immigration advisors.

The Tribunal also has a number of interlocutory powers in respect of both types of cases.

The Tribunal consists of a President who is the judicial head, judicial members who are legally qualified and lay members with experience in the provision of immigration services or in the law and procedures relating to immigration. As at the 31st of December 2005 there was a President, four legally qualified Chairmen and eight lay members.

Hearings are in public (unless the Tribunal directs otherwise). The Tribunal hearing rooms are in London although appeals can be heard wherever appropriate.

The Tribunal's general enquiries number is 020 7029 9790 and the website address is: www.immigrationservicestribunal.gov.uk

Information Tribunal

The Information Tribunal deals with appeals against decisions of the Information Commissioner. Appeals are made under the Data Protection Act (1998) and Freedom of Information Act (2000). The Tribunal also hears National Security Appeals.

The Tribunal is headed by a Chairman who deals with Data Protection and Freedom of Information appeals and National Security cases are handled by the President. They are assisted by nine deputy Chairmen, and a number of lay members.

Table 8.12
The Information Tribunal: cases received and disposed, 2005

	Cases disposed of		
Number of cases received	Heard or determined	Otherwise disposed of	Total disposed of
32	10	7	17

The general enquiries number is 0845 6000877.

Lands Tribunal

The Lands Tribunal was set up in 1949 in order to resolve disputes about land, both as an appellate body and as a tribunal of first instance. The main jurisdictions are –

- Disputed valuations in relation to the compulsory purchase of land or property.
- Claims for compensation for loss of value arising from public works.
- Discharge and modification of restrictive covenants.
- Appeals against decisions of Leasehold Valuation Tribunals.
- Appeals against decisions of Valuation Tribunals.

The Tribunal comprises a full-time legal President, together with three full-time surveyor members and one part-time legal member.

Tribunal hearings usually consist of a single member sitting alone although more complex cases may require two or three members. The President of the Tribunal must have been a judge or a barrister, and other members must be either lawyers or persons experienced in the valuation of land.

The Lands Tribunal's jurisdictions cover England and Wales and the majority of hearings are heard at the Tribunal's hearing centre in London although cases may be heard wherever is appropriate. The Tribunal also has the power to award costs.

Appeals from decisions of the Lands Tribunal lie to the Court of Appeal on a point of law.

Table 8.13
The Immigration Services Tribunal: Appeals and applications received and disposed of, 2005

		Cases disposed of		
	Number of cases received	Heard or determined	Otherwise disposed of	Total
Reference cases:				
Compulsory purchase	164	38	87	125
Land compensation	34	11	19	30
References by consent	5	2	2	4
Blight Notice	9	1	7	8
Other	4	4	2	6
Sub Total	**216**	**56**	**117**	**173**
Law of Property	86	27	33	60
Rights of Light	156	117	7	124
Absent Owners	21	40	1	41
Appellate jurisdictions				
Leasehold Reform Appeals	147	24	23	47
Rating Appeals:				
up to £50,000	74	26	17	43
over £50,000	0	10	4	14
Sub Total	**221**	**60**	**44**	**104**
Grand Total	**700**	**300**	**202**	**502**

The Tribunal's general enquiries number is 020 7029 9790 and the website address is: www.landstribunal.gov.uk

Pensions Appeal Tribunals

The Pensions Appeal Tribunals hear appeals from ex-servicemen or women who have had their claims for a War Pension rejected by the Secretary of State for Defence. The Tribunals' jurisdiction covers England and Wales (Scotland and Northern Ireland have their own Tribunals) and they are independent from the Veterans Agency.

The Pensions Appeal Tribunals deal with appeals concerning –

- An appellant's entitlement to a war pension
- The percentage the Veterans Agency has assessed an appellant's disability
- Whether an appellant is entitled to one of the allowances that supplement a war pension.

- The backdating of the date from which a pension was awarded.
- Whether compensation from a third party is reasonable.
- The Armed Forces Compensation Scheme (from April 2005)

The Pensions Appeal Tribunals are headed by a legally qualified President and Deputy President. The appeal hearings are heard by a panel comprising of a part-time Legal Chairman, Medical Member and a Service Member. As at 31st December 2005 there were 24 legal chairmen, 38 medical members and 32 service members.

The Tribunal has hearing centres covering England and Wales, and these are situated in London, Birmingham, Bradford, Manchester, North Shields and Newport with satellite centres in Plymouth and Taunton. Their jurisdiction is to deal with the cases of appellants resident in England and Wales and outside the UK.

Travelling and subsistence expenses are reimbursed to appellants, as are medical expenses authorised by the Tribunal, but no legal costs are awarded.

The introduction of the Armed Forces (Pensions and Compensation) Act, which came into force in April 2005, changed the avenue of appeals, so that appeals lodged on or after the 6 April 2005 are no longer heard by the High Court but by the Commissioners' Office, who for the purposes of these cases are known as Pensions Appeal Commissioners.

Table 8.14
The Pensions Appeal Tribunals: Appeals received and disposed of in England and Wales, 2005

	Cases disposed of		
Number of cases received	Heard or determined	Otherwise disposed of	Total
2,850	2,576	164	**2,740**

The Tribunal's general enquiries number is 020 7029 9818 and the website address is: www.pensionsappealtribunals.gov.uk

The General Commissioners

The General Commissioners are an independent tribunal constituted by the Taxes Management Act 1970 (as amended by subsequent Finance Acts). General Commissioners are appointed by the Lord Chancellor (or, in Scotland, by the Scottish Ministers) to local Divisions. There are currently 392 Divisions.

Table 8.15
The Commissioners' Office: Applications and appeals received and disposed of in England and Wales, 2005

		Cases disposed of		
	Number of cases received	Heard or determined	Otherwise disposed of	Total Disposed
Applications:	3,739	3,767	102	3,869
Appeals:	1,858	1,972	30	2,002
Total	**5,597**	**5,739**	**132**	**5,871**

Transport Tribunal

The Transport Tribunal was set up in accordance with the Transport Act 1985 to hear and decide appeals against decisions of Traffic Commissioners. These appeals concern operators of road vehicles (both heavy goods and public service vehicles) and the premises which are used as operating centres for the vehicles. An operator may also apply to the Tribunal for a decision of a Commissioner to be stayed (i.e. deferred). Since April 2002 the Transport Tribunal has the additional jurisdiction which considers appeals against decisions of the Registrar of Approved Driving Instructors. The Tribunal also oversees the resolution of disputes under the Postal Services Act 2000 and the Tribunal members also form the London Service Permit Appeal Panel which hears appeals from Transport for London.

The Tribunal is a Court of Record, and its jurisdictions cover England, Scotland and Wales. The tribunal consists of a President, three legal Chairmen and six lay Members all of whom have experience in transport operations and its law and procedures.

There are Tribunal hearing rooms in London and Edinburgh although appeals can be heard wherever appropriate.

Appeals against the decisions of the Tribunal may be made only on a point of law to either the Court of Appeal or the Court of Session in Scottish cases.

The Tribunal's general enquiries number is 020 7029 9790 and the website address is: www.transporttribunal.gov.uk

Table 8.16
The Transport Tribunal: Appeals and Applications received and disposed of, 2005

		Cases disposed of		
	Number of cases received	Heard or determined	Otherwise disposed of	Total
Appeals:				
Traffic Commissioner cases	124	96	30	128
Driving Instructor cases	472	208	218	426
Total Appeals	**596**	**304**	**248**	**552**

The Employment Appeal Tribunal

The Employment Appeal Tribunal was constituted by the Employment Protection Act 1975 and is a superior court of record (that is, not subject in any way, save in matters of appeal, to any other court). The Tribunal hears appeals on question of law arising from any decisions of, or any proceedings before, an industrial tribunal. For example, it deals with unfair dismissal and redundancy matters and allegations of discriminatory acts. It may also hear applications for compensation from persons unreasonably excluded from unions. The Tribunal has wide discretion regarding costs. For example, the party against whom the decision has been made may have to pay all or part of the costs of the other party and either party may be penalised if there has been unreasonable delay or conduct on their part. There is a right to appeal from the Tribunal to the Court of Appeal (Civil Division) in England and Wales and to the Court of Session in Scotland.

The Tribunal consists of a High Court Judge, who presides, and normally two other Members who have special knowledge or experience of industrial relations, either as representatives of employers or of workers, and are appointed on the joint recommendation of the Lord Chancellor and the Secretary of State for Employment.

Table 8.17
The Employment Appeal Tribunal: Cases received and disposed of showing class of jurisdiction, 2005

Category	Registered	Withdrawn	Dismissed	Allowed	Remitted	Total
Employment particulars (ERA P1)	35	10	14	4	8	**36**
Protection of wages (ERA P2)	19	4	18	2	8	**32**
Guaranteed payments ERA P3	0	0	1	0	0	**1**
Sunday working/employment protection (ERA P4+5)	0	0	0	0	0	**0**
Time off work (TU) (ERA P6)	2	1	0	0	0	**1**
Maternity rights (ERA P8)	1	0	0	1	1	**2**
Unfair dismissal (ERA P10)	224	53	85	23	48	**209**
Redundancy/insolvency (ERA P11+12)	14	5	8	1	3	**17**
ERA others (ERAORS)	4	2	1	0	1	**4**
Employment TRIB ACT 1996 (ETA)	0	0	0	0	0	**0**
Equal Pay Act (EPA)	23	5	5	6	3	**19**
Sex Discrim Act 1976 (SDA)	40	9	18	11	8	**46**
Race Relations Act 1976 (RRA)	55	7	11	2	16	**36**
TU/LAB Relations Act (TULRA)	11	1	3	2	1	**7**
Disability Discrim Act 1995 (DDA)	48	8	19	9	16	**52**
Trans of undertaking (TUPE)	26	8	10	2	6	**26**
Jurisdiction (JURIS)	27	8	19	9	8	**44**
Interlocutories (INTERLOC)	0	0	1	0	0	**1**
Working Time Regulation (WTR)	21	7	8	2	1	**18**
ET Procedures (ETP)	208	51	55	41	35	**182**
Disc on grounds of Religious Belief (DRB)	2	1	1	0	0	**2**
Others/PIDA	19	5	0	2	1	**8**
National Minimum Wage (NMW)	2	4	1	0	0	**5**
Human Rights Act (HRA)	0	0	0	0	0	**0**
Part Time Workers (PTW)	2	4	0	0	1	**5**
Total	**783**	**193**	**278**	**117**	**165**	**753**

Offices of the Supreme Court

Offices of the Supreme Court include –

- **The Office of Official Solicitor and Public Trustee** – which has a duty to protect the interests of mentally incapacitated adults and children (other than the subject of child welfare proceedings) who are under a legal disability and to act as trustee when there is no-one else suitable to do so

- **The Tipstaff** – whose main responsibility is the execution of warrants and orders issued by Judges throughout all divisions of the Supreme Court Group

- **The Court of Protection** – which is responsible for the management and administration of the property and affairs of persons suffering from mental disability

- **The Public Guardianship Office** – which deals with private monies either held in court pending a court case, or in trust, or on behalf of the mentally disabled

- **Court Funds Office** – involves receiving, holding and paying out money paid in satisfaction, awards by courts to minors and certain other sums

During 2005 –

- new referrals increased by almost 47% to 4,237 and active caseload increased by 16% to 5,422 **(Table 9.1)**

- in the Court of Protection, orders made under the Mental Health Act 1983 by Masters, Assistant Masters and nominated officers increased by 21% to 6,654 **(Table 9.3)**

The Public Guardianship Office and Court Funds Office: Estates and Accounts under administration at year end, 1995-2005

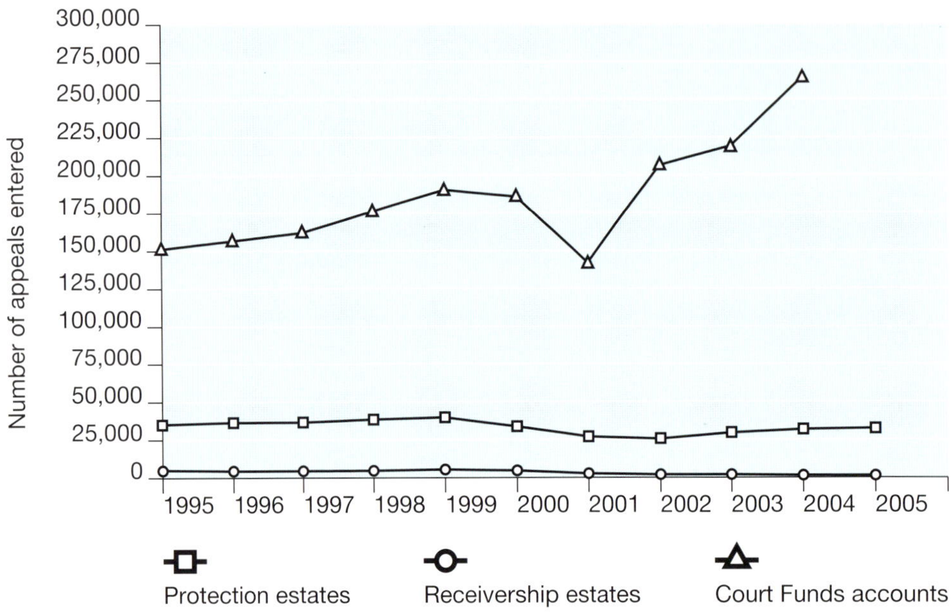

The Office of the Official Solicitor and Trustee

The Official Solicitor (a statutory appointment under section 90 of the Supreme Court Act 1981) acts in legal proceedings for those unable to represent themselves. In particular, he acts for the mentally disabled and children (other than those who are the subject of child welfare proceedings now the responsibility of the Children and Family Court Advisory and Support Service) who are vulnerable litigants because they lack capacity. He will also intervene when there is no-one else able or suitable to do so to prevent an injustice which would arise were he not to act for a party who cannot act for himself. His main objective is to protect the best interests and human rights of those he represents.

In family proceedings he will act as a guardian ad litem of a party suffering from mental disability within the meaning of the Mental Health Act 1983; and in any civil litigation (e.g. personal injury claims, possession actions or applications in connection with inheritances) he will act as the litigation friend of a party under disability when there is no one else suitable or able to do so. He is also brought in to represent incapacitated adults in medical or welfare cases where issues arise as to what lawfully should be done in their best interests. Other cases may involve him representing an estate of a deceased person, usually in circumstances in which there is a need to protect the property of a child or person under mental disability, or some person wishes to claim against an estate for which no personal representative is willing to act. He administers estates and acts as trustee when there is no-one else suitable to do so. He reviews the cases of persons committed to prison for contempt of court. His office represents persons without mental capacity in proceedings concerning their property and affairs before the Court of Protection. He can also be called upon to assist the courts by providing an advocate to the court. From 1 April 2005 the Official Solicitor may be appointed, in place of a parent, to act as the registered contact in the administration of the Government's Child Trust Fund scheme for those children in care in England and Wales where there is no parent able to do so.

His office administers the International Child Abduction and Contact Unit in England and Wales (the Central Authority under the Hague and European Conventions on Child Abduction) to ensure that an aggrieved parent may, with minimal delay, make application to enforce orders in the child's home country, and where the claim is made out secure the return of the child or to pursue access rights. He also (since 1 April 2005) administers the Reciprocal Enforcement Maintenance Order (REMO) Unit which acts for the Lord Chancellor as the Central Authority for England & Wales for international maintenance claims, i.e. claims where one of the parties lives outside the United Kingdom in one of the 100 or so countries and territories that have reciprocal arrangements with the UK in this area.

In 2005 noteworthy cases in which the Official Solicitor was involved included the following –

- **W Healthcare NHS Trust v H and Others:** The OS represented a 59 year old woman who had suffered from multiple sclerosis for 20 years. She lived in a nursing home and required 24 hour care. She had been fed through a percutaneous gastrostomy tube (PEG) for 5 years. In August 2004 the tube fell out and she was admitted to hospital. It was the unanimous view of the treating clinicians that the tube should be reinserted, but the family did not want this to happen since they believed that in the circumstances she would rather die. The Hospital Trust, supported by the OS, sought a declaration that H lacked capacity to make a decision about reinsertion of the PEG tube and that in the circumstances it was in her best interests for the PEG to be reinserted. The Judge at first instance held that there was no clear expression of the patient's wishes that would amount to an advance directive. In the circumstances the court held that it was in H's best interests for the PEG to be reinserted and made the declaration sought. The Court of Appeal upheld the decision on the same day.

- **Lewis v Gibson:** The OS intervened in an appeal by Mrs Lewis against an order of the county court removing her as nearest relative of her daughter, the order being made on grounds that she unreasonably objected to her daughter being made the subject of a guardianship order under the Mental Health Act. The patient had not been represented in the county court, because the Rules expressly prevented her from being a party. The OS made submissions, accepted by the Court of Appeal, that, the rule having been amended to allow the patient to be a party (following representations to the Rule Committee by the OS) it was good practice in all cases for the court to notify the patient or a litigation friend on her behalf of the proceedings and the right to be joined as a party to those proceedings.

The Public Trustee, appointed under the Public Trustee Act 1906, acts as executor or administrator of deceased persons' estates or trustee of wills or settlements, when nominated to do so and he accepts that nomination. Increasingly, since the policy changes announced by the Lord Chancellor in April 2000 in "Making Changes – the Future of the Public Trust Office", this function is concentrating upon providing a public sector service of last resort where there is a social need for the Public Trustee to act which could not be met in the private sector. Since 1 April 2001, as also announced in that policy statement, the office has been combined with that of the Official Solicitor following the appointment of the same individual to the two statutory offices

Table 9.1
Supreme Court – Office of the Official Solicitor and Public Trustee: cases accepted and carried forward, 2005

Official Solicitor	New Referrals	Average Monthly Active cases
Family Litigation	823	800
Medical/Welfare	89	34
Divorce	175	525
Civil Litigation	726	1,111
Court of Protection	618	565
Bails/Contempts	273	72
Child Abduction	402	311
REMO	777	n/a
Child Trust Funds	341	n/a
Estates	12	695
Public Trustee		
Trusts & Executorships	1	1,302
Pension & Institutional Funds	–	7
Total	**4,237**	**5,422**

Tipstaff

The Tipstaff is appointed under section 27 of the Courts Act 1971, a general provision which enables the Lord Chancellor to appoint officers and other staff in the Supreme Court and county courts.

The duties of the Tipstaff are many and varied but broadly the Tipstaff is the enforcement officer for all issues falling within the jurisdiction of England and Wales. The principal areas of specific duties emanate from the Queens Bench, Chancery and Family Divisions and involve issues of Bankruptcy, Insolvency, Wardship, Contempt of Court, Writ Ne Exeat Regno (no exit from this jurisdiction) and many other miscellaneous orders which involve taking action to enforce, or prevent breach of, orders of the Court.

About 80% of the Tipstaff's work is in the Family Division and usually involves a missing or abducted child. In these cases a Collection Order (return of a child) or a Location Order (the whereabouts of a child discovered) is granted. When the child's whereabouts is known, but there is a fear that there could be a removal from the jurisdiction, a Passport Order could be asked for, seizing certain passports and/or travel documents thus preventing a wrongful removal.

At the moment there is one Tipstaff, with one deputy and three assistants to cover England and Wales, and they are based at the Royal Courts of Justice in London.

During 2005, 11 persons were conveyed to prison by the Tipstaff or his assistants, 18 fewer than in 2004. In 2005, 380 warrants were executed (334 in 2004) and 46 warrants were suspended, discharged or expired.

Table 9.2
Supreme Court – Tipstaff: warrants dealt with, 2005

Warrants issued by	Warrants executed	Persons Conveyed	Warrants suspended or discharged
Chancery Division	6	1	–
Queen's Bench Division	8	6	1
Bankruptcy	5	2	10
Insolvency	–	–	11
Family Division	28	2	5
Collection/Location/Seizure/			
of passports Orders[1]	322	–	18
Port Alert Orders	11	–	1
Total	380	11	46

[1] Includes previous editions Child Abduction category

Court of Protection

The Court of Protection is an office of the Supreme Court which exercises judicial functions in respect of the property and financial affairs of persons who are incapable, by reason of mental disorder, of managing and administering their own property and affairs. Such persons are technically known as *patients*.

The Court's powers are conferred by the Mental Health Act 1983, Enduring Power of Attorney Act 1985, the Court of Protection Rules 2001, and the Court of Protection (Enduring Powers of Attorneys) Rules 2001.

These powers are exercisable by the Lord Chancellor, nominated judges [the judges of the Chancery Division and (since 5th May 2000) the judges of the Family Division], the Master, Assistant Masters and other nominated officers of the Court of Protection.

Certain orders can only be made by the Lord Chancellor or a nominated judge but, subject to these exceptions, the jurisdiction is in practice exercised by the other people mentioned.

In 2005 there was one order made by a nominated judge (four in 2004) with 6,654 orders being made by the Master, Assistant Masters or nominated officers (5,481 in 2004).

The Court of Protection approved 384 damages awards in 2005.

Of these, 162 (42%) were in respect of road traffic accidents, with average date of birth of the claimant being August 1977, and the average date of the accident September 1999.

140 (37%) were for clinical negligence, with the average date of birth of the claimant being February 1992. 93 (66%) of the clinical negligence cases were for birth or perinatal injuries. The take-up rate for periodical payments, rather than a conventional lump sum, was over 26%.

Of the other 82 cases, 16 were awards made by the Criminal Injuries Compensation Authority, nine were damages for sexual or physical abuse suffered whilst the claimant was in the care of a local authority, 15 were for work injuries, and the remaining 42 cases were for a miscellaneous variety of accidents.

Since 1 October 2001, to make the Court more accessible to the public by providing it with regional presence, a district judge sitting as a part-time Deputy Master of the Court of Protection has heard contentious matters at Preston Combined Court Centre.

Table 9.3
Supreme Court – Court of Protection: Proceedings under the Mental Health Act 1983 and the Enduring Powers of Attorney Act 1985, 2005

Nature of Proceedings	
Orders made on first applications under the Mental Health Act 1983 by Master, Assistant Masters and nominated officers	6,654
Orders made on subsequent applications	789
Orders made by a nominated judge	1
Orders for sale and purchase of property	1,934
Wills executed for clients and sealed with the Court's seal and orders for settlement and gifts, excluding those made on applications relating to Enduring Powers of Attorney	329
Orders made on applications relating to Enduring Powers of Attorney dealt with by the Judicial Support Unit Department	394
Applications for orders appointing new trustees under sections 36(9), 54 and 96(1)(k) of the Trustee Act 1925 and section 20(2)(c) of the Trusts of Land and Appointment of Trustees Act 1996	523
Orders determining proceedings on a patient's recovery	68
Visits carried out by the Lord Chancellor's medical visitors	105

The Public Guardianship Office

The Public Guardianship Office (PGO) was established as an executive Agency on 2 April 2001. The agency as part of the Court of Protection, undertakes the Mental Health functions previously carried out by the Public Trust Office.

The PGO provides an integrated service for its clients, safeguarding their financial interest while avoiding unnecessary state intervention. Its major function is to protect and promote the interests of its clients by overseeing and supporting the activities of Receivers appointed by the Court of Protection to manage their financial affairs. Where the Court of Protection adjudges a person mentally incapable of managing their own financial affairs, and there is no one else willing or suitable to act as Receiver, the PGO will appoint one of the professionals from the panel of Receivers to act on behalf of that person. In exceptional cases if no one can be appointed as Receiver the PGO will take the role itself. In addition, the PGO carries out the administrative functions arising from the Court of Protection's jurisdiction under the Enduring Powers of Attorney Act 1985.

At the end of 2005 the agency was protecting the affairs of some 31,140 Protection Division clients. It was also directly managing the affairs of 145 Receivership clients. The agency was responsible for approximately £3.5 billion of clients' funds.

Table 9.4
The Public Guardianship Office: Matters under administration, 2005

Nature of Proceedings	
Protection Work:	
Estates under adminstration:	
At year start	30,471
Total applications brought in during year	9,242
At year end	31,140
Annual accounts and enquiries passed	13,664
Short Orders issued	2,044
Schedules (other than orders) for dealing with funds	26,746
Lodgement schedules (other than orders) for payment into Court	4,750
Enduring Powers of Attorney:	
Applications received during year	19,776
Number registered during year	20,003
Total remaining registered during year	100,221
Receivership Work:	
Estates under adminstration at year start	239
Estates under adminstration at year end	154

Estimated value of funds under adminstration was £3.5 billion

Court Funds Office

Court Funds Office transferred to the Supreme Court Group of the Court Service on the 1 April 2001. Court Funds work involves receiving, holding and paying out money paid in satisfaction, awards by Courts to minors, money held on behalf of Public Guardianship Office, Protection and Receivership clients and certain other sums.

It manages money held in court on behalf of clients who may –

- be involved in a civil legal action
- be patients who, under the Court of Protection, are not able to manage their property and affairs
- be Children under the age of 18

These are non-agency assets and are not included in the accounts. The assets held at the balance sheet date comprised cash, securities and Index Tracker Funds.

The accounts relating to Court Funds are published annually in a parliamentary White Paper with 28th February being the end of financial year. Further information regarding the Court Funds Office can be found on this site; www.hmcourts-service.gov.uk/infoabout/cfo/index.htm.

The Judiciary

Divisional Heads
The four Heads of Division are –

- the Lord Chief Justice of England – the senior judicial officer in England and Wales. He heads the Queen's Bench Division of the High Court and also the criminal branch of the Court of Appeal

- the Master of the Rolls, who heads the civil branch of the Court of Appeal

- the President of the Family Division

- the Vice-Chancellor, heads the Chancery Division which handles cases involving large sums of money and nationally important legal financial issues

Lords Justices
Together with the Lord Chief Justice and the Master of the Rolls, the Lords Justices are judges of the Court of Appeal. As at 1 January 2006 there were 37 Lords Justices in office.

High Court Judges
As at 1 January 2006 there were 107 High Court judges in office. 17 were assigned to the Chancery Division (Chapter 2), 72 to the Queen's Bench Division (Chapter 3) and 18 to the Family Division (Chapter 5).

Circuit and District Judges
The numbers of circuit and district judges, and part-time recorders sitting at 1 January 2006 are shown in Table 9.1.

During 2005 –

- 34 additional circuit judges were put in post throughout England and Wales although there were 55 recorders and 3 district judges fewer **(Table 9.1)**

- at 26%, London (including the Royal Courts of Justice) accounted for the highest proportion of days sat by all judges in England and Wales (66,451) **(Table 9.3)**

- 1,739 lay magistrates were appointed while the total in England and Wales fell by over 1% to 28,253

In the Court of Appeal a bench of two or three judges sits on each case. In the Criminal Division the bench consists of the Lord Chief Justice or a Lord Justice and one or more, usually two High, Court judges. In the Civil Division the majority of cases are heard by a bench solely composed of Lords Justices.

The bulk of Crown Court work is undertaken by circuit judges and recorders. In the county courts most of the work is undertaken by circuit judges, district judges and deputy district judges.

District Judges (Magistrates' Courts)

There were 124 district judges (magistrates' courts) in post at 1 January 2006. They are appointed by the Queen on the recommendation of the Lord Chancellor. Their role is to support the lay magistracy and to deal with the full range of cases which come before the lay bench. They are entitled to sit with lay magistrates or to sit alone.

Justices of the peace

Justices of the peace (lay magistrates) are appointed by the Lord Chancellor on behalf of the Sovereign, except in Greater Manchester, Merseyside and Lancashire where appointments are made by the Chancellor to the Duchy of Lancaster.

In the magistrates' court the justices usually sit as a bench of three: when sitting as a Youth Court or Family Proceedings Court there must be at least one male and one female justice on the bench.

In the Crown Court justices sit with a judge to hear appeals and cases committed from magistrates' courts for sentence.

Judges Sitting Days (All courts), 1995-2005

(deputies/assistants are included in each category)

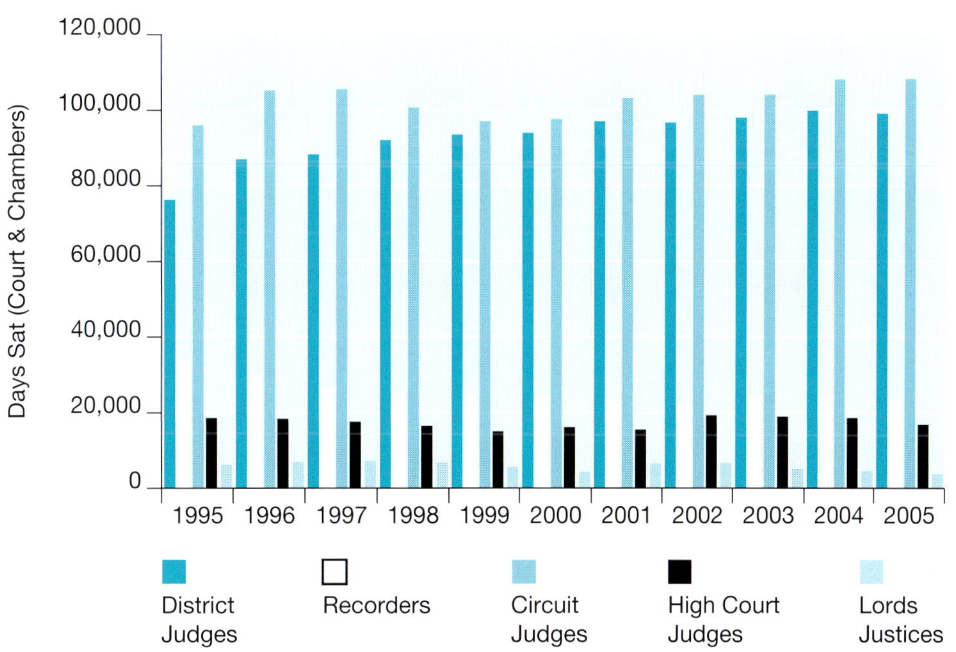

Justices of the Peace, 1995-2005*

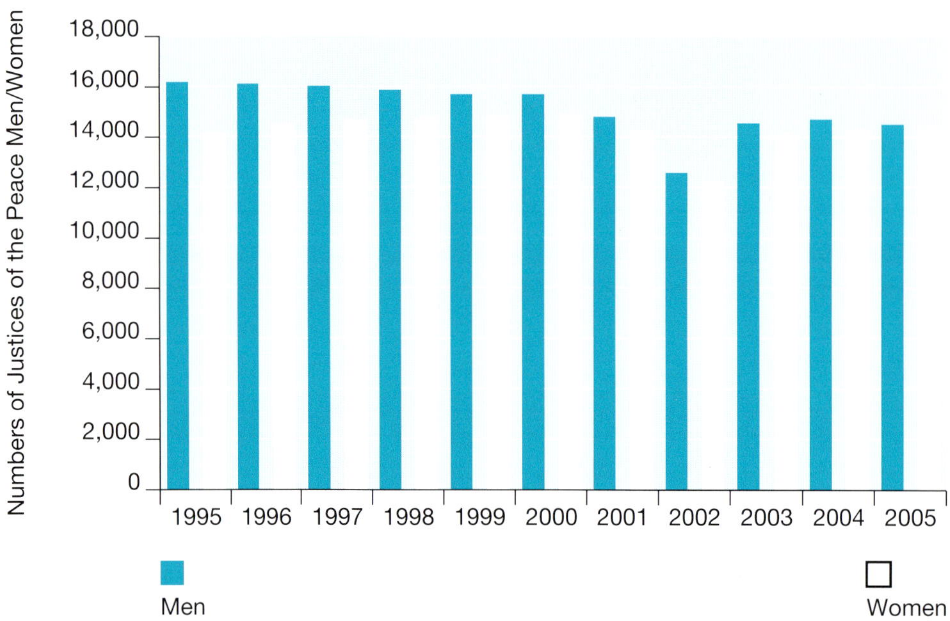

* As at 1st January of each year. From 2000 onwards figures compiled on a financial year basis.

Judges

At 1 January 2006, just over 42% of circuit judges and recorders were assigned to the South Eastern circuit. There are 622 circuit judges, an decrease of over 3% on the previous year.

The number of district judges in post has decreased by 3 to 421.

Table 10.1
Circuit judges, recorders and district judges in post in each circuit at 1 January 2005

Circuit	Circuit Judges	Recorders	District Judges
Midlands	87	226	63
North East	77	145	61
North West	88	177	64
South East	270	581	152
South West	61	179	49
Wales and Cheshire	39	89	32
England & Wales	**622**	**1,397**	**421**

Table 9.2 shows the number of days sat by each category of judge according to the type of work undertaken, while Table 9.3 shows the distribution of days sat by circuit. Sittings by deputy High Court judges include retired Lords Justices, retired High Court judges and circuit judges sitting as High Court judges under section 9(1) of the Supreme Court Act 1981 and Queen's Counsel sitting as deputy High Court judges under section 9(4) of the Act. Deputy circuit judge sittings refer only to sittings by retired circuit judges.

In 2005 a total of 251,570 days were sat by judges on all types of work (excluding tribunals and other official functions) with days sat in the Crown Court (93,526) accounting for 37%. Total days in the county court and the High Court accounted for 55% and nearly 6% respectively. The remaining 5,120 days were sat in the Court of Appeal.

Circuit judges sat nearly 43% of all days during 2005, Lords Justices accounted for over 1%, High Court judges nearly 3%, deputy High Court judges just over 1%, deputy circuit judges nearly 1%, recorders over 9%, district judges nearly 31% and deputy district judges nearly 9%.

In the Crown Court circuit judges sat just over 74% of days while recorders accounted for nearly 20%. Of the days sat on county court work circuit judges sat over 24%, with district judges and deputy district judges accounting nearly 72%.

Table 10.2

Days sat[1] by judges showing type of work dealt with, 2005

	Court of Appeal		High Court				Crown Court	County Court			
	Criminal	Civil	Chancery Division	Queen's Bench Division[2]	Family Division	T&C court		General List	Family Law Public	Family Law Private	Total
Type of judge											
Lords Justices	720	2,666	42	135	58	15	–	55	24	51	3,766
High Court judges	1,230	91	2,081	3,378	2,244	380	3,886	41	161	73	13,563
Deputy High Court judges	108	109	1,098	929	399	267	185	90	112	15	3,311
Circuit judges	196	–	940	717	1,224	790	69,630	11,859	13,707	7,127	106,190
Deputy circuit judges	–	–	1	13	1	–	1,098	459	321	202	2,094
Recorders	–	–	29	3	84	11	18,727	3,124	408	1,102	23,487
District judges	–	–	301	176	2	–	–	51,615	2,473	22,797	77,362
Deputy district judges	–	–	6	2	1	–	–	18,768	77	2,945	21,798
Total[4]	**2,254**	**2,866**	**4,497**	**5,351**	**4,012**	**1,463**	**86,010**	**17,282**	**34,311**	**251,570**	**251,570**

[1] Days sat in court and chambers

[2] Admiralty Court and Administrative Court sittings are included in the Queen's Bench Division figures

[3] T&C court – Technology and Construction Court, formally the Official Referee's court

[4] These figures represent only the days sat in court or in chambers in the jurisdictions shown. Judges sit in other areas, and also undertake a range of other functions outside the courtroom that are not shown here

Table 10.3

Days sat[1] by judges, by type of judge and circuit, 2005

Type of judge	London	Midlands	North East	North West	South East	South West	Supreme Court	Wales & Cheshire	Grand Total
Lords Justices	36	43	3	11	31	16	3,627	–	3,766
High Court judges	574	1,174	724	1,404	535	364	8,262	527	13,563
Deputy High Court judges	164	933	178	426	21	74	1,250	266	3,311
Circuit judges	26,509	15,252	11,148	15,015	19,810	8,715	2,434	7,309	106,190
Deputy circuit judges	395	42	128	265	819	281	1	164	2,094
Recorders	5,960	3,931	2,591	2,627	4,119	2,526	88	1,646	23,487
District judges	12,604	11,463	11,024	11,879	15,633	8,894	–	5,866	77,362
Deputy district judges	2,591	3,665	3,257	4,032	3,924	2,719	–	1,611	21,798
Total[3]	**48,833**	**36,503**	**29,053**	**35,657**	**44,889**	**23,587**	**15,662**	**17,388**	**251,570**

[1] Days sat in court and chambers

[2] Includes the Royal Courts of Justice

[3] These figures represent only the days sat in court or in chambers in the jurisdictions shown. Judges sit in other areas, and also undertake a range of other functions outside the courtroom that are not shown here

County Courts: Days sat, 2005

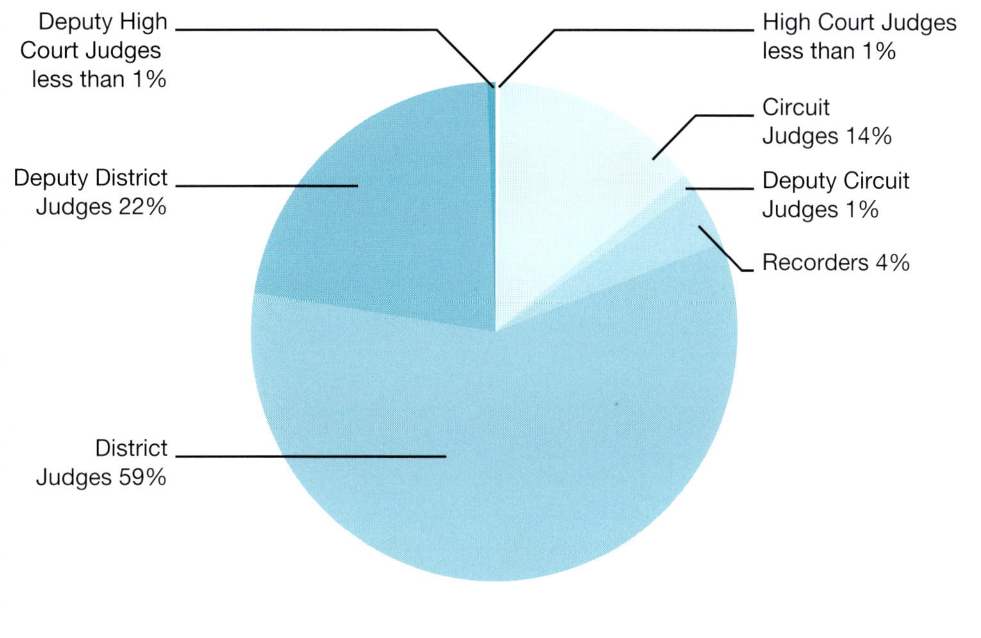

Court of Appeal: Days sat, 2005

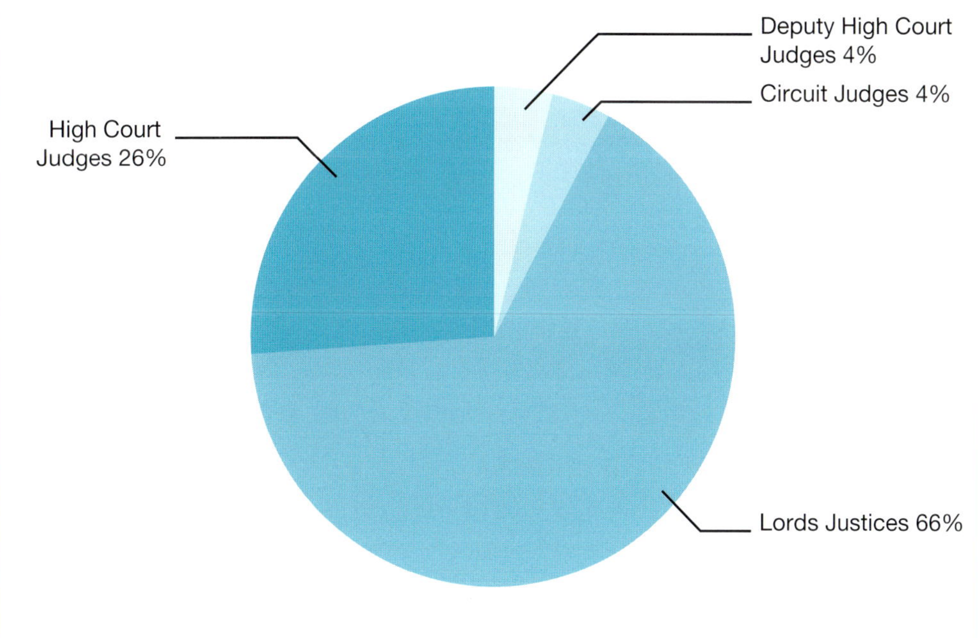

High Courts: Days sat, 2005

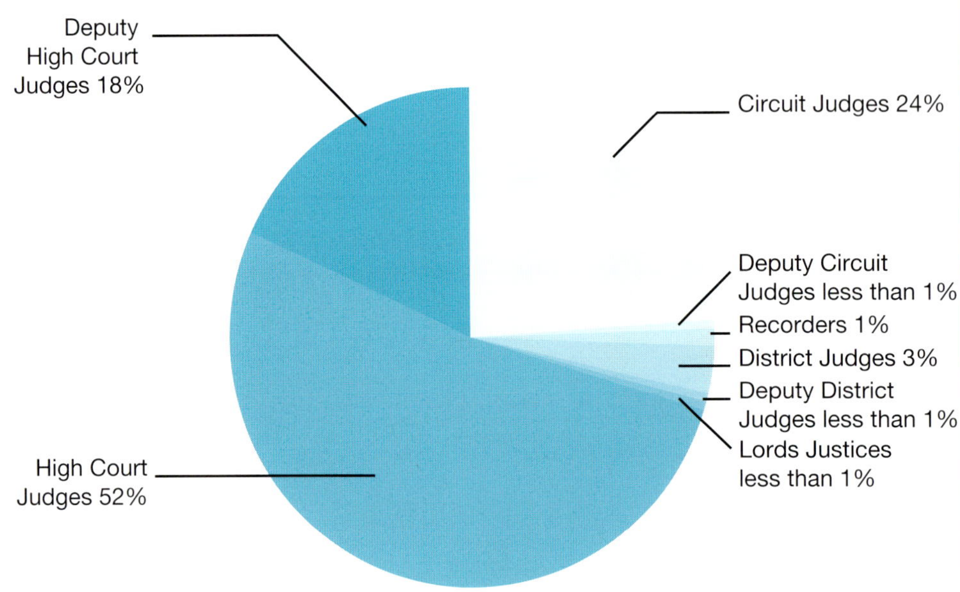

Crown Court: Days sat, 2005

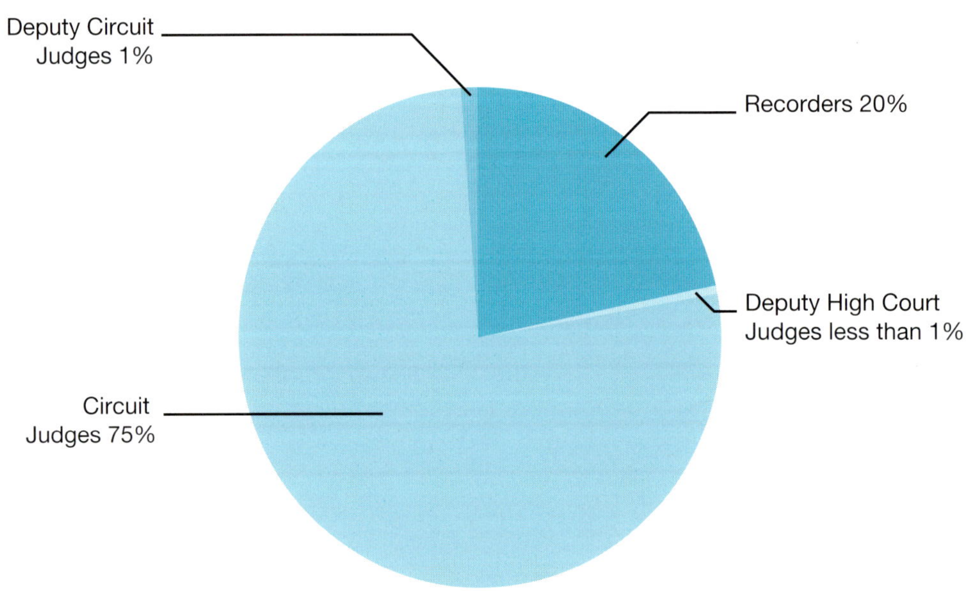

The Lay Magistracy

The Lord Chancellor appoints justices on the advice of committees which have been set up throughout England and Wales. It is the aim of both the Lord Chancellor and the Chancellor of the Duchy of Lancaster that once suitability has been established each bench of magistrates should broadly reflect the community it serves.

Most of the work of justices is done in court – mainly a magistrates' court (including the Youth Court and Family Proceedings Court) – and in the Crown Court. About 98% of all criminal cases are dealt with by magistrates. The bulk of these are purely summary offences which can only be tried in a magistrates' court and include motoring offences. The remainder are 'either way' offences which may be tried either in the magistrates' court or in the Crown Court before a judge and jury.

Criminal cases involving children and young persons up to and including the age of 17 are normally dealt with in the Youth Court (prior to October 1992, this was known as the Juvenile Court and dealt with children and young persons up to the age of 16). Justices sitting in the Family Proceedings Court deal with the court's family business, such as cases concerning children and young persons who are believed to be in need of care, matters concerning residence and contact with children and maintenance (see chapter 5).

The names of justices of the peace who reach the compulsory retiring age of 70 may be transferred to the Supplemental List and thereafter perform limited functions such as signing any document for the purpose of authenticating another person's signature. Unlike district judges (magistrates' court), lay magistrates are unpaid but many receive certain allowances to cover travelling expenses, subsistence and financial loss occasioned by the performance of their duties.

Table 10.4
Justices of peace in England and Wales[1] as at 1 April 2005[2] and selected years since 1978

Year	Total	Men	Women
1978	23,483	14,633	8,850
1988	27,926	15,992	11,934
1990	28,667	16,090	12,577
1991	29,062	16,098	12,964
1992	29,441	16,105	1,336
1993	29,686	16,087	13,599
1994	30,054	16,151	13,903
1995	30,088	16,045	14,043
1996	30,326	15,951	14,375
1997	30,374	15,858	14,516
1998	30,361	15,713	14,648
1999	30,260	15,561	14,699
2000	30,308	15,544	14,764
2001[2]	28,735	14,639	14,096
2002[2]	24,526	12,439	12,087
2003[2]	28,344	14,392	13,952
2004[2]	28,705	14,555	14,150
2005[2]	28,253	14,256	13,997
2006[2]	28,865	14,519	14,346

[1] Including the Duchy of Lancaster

[2] Figures are now compiled on a financial year basis

At 1 April 2005 there was a total of 28,865 justices of the peace in England and Wales, over 1% more than a year previously. Of the total, 14,519 (over 50%) were men and 14,346 (over 49%) were women. During 2005/06, 1,132 men and 1,080 women were appointed justices of the peace.

Table 10.5
Justices of peace appointed[1] since 1990

Year	Total	Men	Women
1990	2,059	996	1,063
1991	2,017	1,008	1,009
1992	2,070	1,080	990
1993	2,062	1,045	1,017
1994	1,593	810	783
1995	1,843	907	936
1996	1,682	830	852
1997	1,573	764	809
1998	1,609	816	793
1999	1,743	884	859
2001[2]	1,618	834	784
2002[2]	1,474	763	711
2003[2]	1,623	838	785
2004[2]	1,807	1,002	805
2005[2, 3]	1,739	892	847
2006[2]	2,212	1,132	1,080

[1] England and Wales including the Duchy of Lancaster

[2] Figures are now compiled on a financial year basis

[3] Some appointments data was not available at the time of collection and is not included

Note: In July 2005 a new database was implemented. Prior to the 05/06 year, figures were collected manually from Advisory Committee annual reports due in that financial year regardless of the appointment date. From 05/06 onwards, figures are collated according to the date of appointment to the Local Justice Area within the financial year.

District Judges (Magistrates' Courts)

Unification of the Stipendiary Bench took place following the implementation on 31 August 2000 of Section 78 of the Access to Justice Act 1999. The unification of the bench created a national jurisdiction throughout England and Wales and a change of title from Stipendiary Magistrates to District Judges (Magistrates' Courts). There is a single judicial head, the Senior District Judge (Chief Magistrate), who is responsible for the administration of the unified bench.

There were 134 full-time district judges (magistrates' courts) in post at 1 January 2006. They are appointed by the Queen on the recommendation of the Lord Chancellor. They are full-time members of the judiciary and deal with a broad range of business that comes before the magistrates' courts but in particular may be expected to hear the lengthier and more complex criminal matters coming before those courts. They are entitled to sit with lay magistrates or to sit alone.

Publicly Funded Legal Services and Taxation of Costs

The Administration of Publicly Funded Legal Services

The Legal Services Commission (which replaced the Legal Aid Board in April 2000) is responsible to the Lord Chancellor for the administration of civil and family publicly funded legal services and all criminal public funding below the Crown Court.

Civil Funding

Access to publicly funded civil and family legal services in England and Wales is provided through the Community Legal Service, administered by the Legal Services Commission. The different levels of service provided are –

i) **Legal Help** – this provides initial advice and assistance with legal problems and covers work previously carried out under the 'green form' scheme

ii) **Help at Court** – this allows for somebody (a solicitor or adviser) to speak on behalf of a person at certain court hearings, without formally acting for that person in the whole proceedings

iii) **Approved Family Help** – this provides help in relation to a family dispute, including assistance in resolving that dispute through negotiation or otherwise. This includes the services covered by Legal Help, but also includes issuing proceedings and representation where necessary to obtain disclosure of information from another party, or to obtain a consent order following an agreement of matters in dispute. It is available in two forms –

Help with Mediation: legal advice and assistance if a person is attending family mediation

General Family Help: legal advice and assistance on family matters where a person is not attending family mediation

iv) **Family Mediation** – this level of service covers mediation for a family dispute, including finding out whether mediation appears suitable or not

v) **Legal Representation** – this level of service provides legal representation so that a person can be represented in court if taking or defending proceedings. This is the same level of service previously called civil legal aid. It is available in two forms:

Investigative Help: funding is limited to investigation of the strength of a claim

Full Representation: funding is provided to represent people in legal proceedings

vi) **Support Funding** – this provides partial funding of very expensive cases which are otherwise funded privately. It is available in two forms:

Investigative Support: funding is limited to investigation of the strength of a claim with a view to a conditional fee agreement

Litigation Support: provides partial funding of high cost proceedings under a conditional fee agreement

The availability of funding will normally be restricted to those who qualify on financial grounds ('the means test') and who can satisfy the Legal Services Commission that funding should be made available in the particular circumstances of the case. The Commission's 'Funding Code' describes the various circumstances. A person who is entitled to funding may be called upon to make a contribution towards the cost of a case depending on their financial circumstances.

Detailed Assessment of Costs in Civil Proceedings
The detailed assessment of costs is the process of examining and if, necessary, reducing the bill of costs of a solicitor or Litigant in Person. Costs include not only the solicitor's own professional fees, but also disbursements incurred including barristers'and experts' fees. The purpose of detailed assessment is –

a) to determine how much costs a successful party in litigation is entitled to recover from his unsuccessful opponent

b) in publicly funded cases to determine the amount which a solicitor or barrister is to be paid out of public funds

c) under the Solicitors' Act to determine how much a client should have to pay his solicitor.

The office responsible for assessing costs depends on the type of case and whether it is publicly funded. The Supreme Court Costs Office (SCCO) deals mainly with costs relating to all proceedings in the Chancery, Family and Queen's Bench Divisions of the High Court, the Court of Appeal (Civil Division) and the London County Court Group. It also deals with costs in matters involving the Court of Protection, various tribunals and assessments transferred from other county courts and district registries. It also deals with appeals against the determination of costs in the Crown Court. The Privy Council, House of Lords, Lands Tribunal, and, except as above, district registries and county courts are responsible for the detailed assessment of costs in their respective courts.

In 2005, the SCCO assessed 13,772 bills as against to 13,397 in 2004. The number of between parties' assessments of bills of costs in civil cases showed a reduction of 7.5% due in part to the impact of Predictable Costs in Road Traffic Cases. Court of Protection assessments increased by a further

36% resulting in an overall increase of 2.8% in cases assessed. The substantial increase in Court of Protection assessments has been brought mainly about by the withdrawal of agreed costs resulting in more bills requiring formal assessment. A random sample over four years (2002-2005) of completed between parties' assessments shows an average reduction of 23.6%.

The following table shows a breakdown of the type of bill assessed in the Supreme Court Costs Office.

Type of assessment	Number Assessed in 2005
Between Parties Assessments	3,062
Receivers' Costs in the Court of Protection	4,438
Appeals from Crown Court Determining Officers	333
Civil Legal Aid	5,939

Table 11.1

Taxation of Costs : Bills taxed under headings shown, amounts brought in and allowed, and average amounts at which bills were allowed, 2005

	Number of bills taxed	Brought in at (£)	Allowed at (£)	Average amount at which bills were allowed (£)
Judicial Committee of the Privy Council:				
Petitions for special leave	5	32,868.71	33,236.91	6,647.40
Appeals	10	573,502.53	342,525.62	34,352.60
House of Lords:				
Petitions for leave	25	144,756	108,263	4,330
Petitions of appeal	24	1,744,630	1,235,405	51,475
Supreme Court Costs Office[1]				
Administrative Court	–	–	..	..
Chancery Division	–	–	..	..
Court of Appeal	–	–	..	..
Court of Protection	–	–	..	..
Family Division	–	–	..	..
Queen's Bench	–	–	..	..
Other Tribunals	–	–	..	..
From County Courts	–	–	..	..
Appeals for Crown Court in Criminal Cases	–	–	–	–
Lands Tribunal	**4**	**213,456**	**164,504**	**41,126**

[1] Amounts allowed: a random sample of civil cases where detailed assessment was completed in 2004 showed that bills were reduced by an average of 20%. Over a three-year sample (2002-2004) the average is 23.7%.

Criminal Public Funding

The Criminal Defence Service (CDS) was introduced in April 2001 – it replaced the old legal aid scheme.

Advice and assistance is available to individuals who are arrested and held in custody at a police station or other premises and for individuals who are involved in criminal investigations, without reference to their financial resources. Advocacy assistance is also available without reference to a defendant's means for individuals appearing before a magistrates' court or the Crown Court.

An accused person can have publicly funded representation where the court decides that it is in the interests of justice to do so. A representation order covers all criminal proceedings; preliminary or incidental including any related bail proceedings. Where a defendant has a representation order in a magistrates' court or the Crown Court, the representation order covers obtaining advice on appeal and the preparation of any application for leave to appeal or giving notice of appeal against conviction or sentence.

Where a notice of leave to appeal has been given, an application for a further representation order can be made directly to the Court of Appeal to cover those proceedings. Once granted a representation order may provide for a solicitor and in certain cases an advocate, in a magistrates' court or Crown Court.

Where a case is heard in a magistrates' court, no details of the applicant's means are required, as there is no power to recover the cost of the applicant's representation. However, where a case is heard in the Crown Court or a higher court on appeal, the applicant must provide truthful details of his or her means to the court. At the end of the case, the judge has a new power to order the defendant to pay back some or all of the costs of his or her defence, the Recovery of Defence Costs Order. If necessary, the judge will order an investigation of the defendant's means before making the order, where for example further information has come to light. Such enquiries may be undertaken by the Legal Services Commission's Special Investigations Unit, or by the court.

In 2005, 107,664 applications were made in magistrates' courts for representation in the Crown Court and of these virtually all were granted. Similarly, of the 12,639 applications to the Crown Court, nearly all were granted.

Table 11.2

Criminal public funding: Applications[1] filed in the magistrates' courts for representation in the Crown Court, by type of proceeding, 1998-2005

	1998	1999	2000	2001	2002	2003	2004	2005
Trial on indictment:								
Applications	87,741	81,419	79,887	81,864	89,501	89,718	88,277	83,223
Granted	87,734	81,413	79,877	81,860	89,501	89,718	88,277	83,223
Refused	7	6	10	4	–	–	–	–
For sentence or to be dealt with:								
Applications	20,328	21,982	19,110	17,562	19,639	19,511	18,986	20,407
Granted	20,324	21,982	19,110	17,562	19,638	19,511	18,986	20,407
Refused	4	–	–	–	–	–	–	–
Appeals against magistrates' court decision:								
Convictions and sentence:								
Applications	1,382	1,360	1,264	1,240	1,347	1,357	1,397	1,525
Granted	1,382	1,360	1,264	1,239	1,347	1,357	1,397	1,525
Refused	–	–	–	1	–	–	–	–
Sentence only:								
Applications	2,529	2,489	2,557	2,407	2,512	2,484	2,541	2,509
Granted	2,528	2,489	2,557	2,407	2,512	2,484	2,541	2,509
Refused	1	–	–	–	–	–	–	–

[1] Applications granted include a small number of applications granted in the magistrates' courts and extended by the Crown Court. Applications refused include a small number of applications refused in the magistrates' court and later granted by the Crown Court

Table 11.3

Criminal public funding: Applications[1] filed in the Crown Court, by type of proceeding, 1998-2005

	1998	1999	2000	2001	2002	2003	2004	2005
Trial on indictment:								
Applications	6,627	6,173	6,685	6,627	5,310	4,809	4,838	4,768
Granted	6,445	6,011	6,476	6,485	5,152	4,644	4,670	4,582
Refused	182	162	208	162	158	165	168	186
For sentence or to be dealt with:								
Applications	2,626	2,915	3,521	2,583	2,907	3,767	4,554	4,868
Granted	2,604	2,882	3,486	2,561	2,897	3,740	4,532	4,841
Refused	22	33	35	22	10	27	22	27
Appeals against Magistrates court decision:								
Convictions and sentence:								
Applications	1,678	1,424	1,340	1,228	1,273	1,267	1,328	1,380
Granted	1,656	1,401	1,330	1,210	1,256	1,245	1,307	1,359
Refused	22	23	10	18	17	22	21	21
Sentence only:								
Applications	2,079	1,944	1,948	1,655	1,590	1,662	1,656	1,623
Granted	2,067	1,937	1,937	1,653	1,585	1,656	1,651	1,618
Refused	12	7	11	2	5	6	5	5

[1] Applications granted include a small number granted in the magistrates' court and extended by the Crown Court

The percentage of defendants and appellants applying for criminal public funding, the grant rate and thus the percentage represented under criminal public funding varies considerably according to the type of proceeding. A higher percentage of defendants are publicly funded for proceedings in the Crown Court than in magistrates' courts. The majority of defendants appearing at the Crown Court for trial or for sentence are publicly funded (over 94% and almost 80% respectively in 2005).

Table 11.4

Criminal public funding: Defendants and appellants in the Crown Court, by type of proceeding and representation, 2005

	Represented under legal aid	Privately not represented	Total
Trial on indictment	85,851	5,271	91,122
For sentence or to be dealt with	25,001	6,205	31,206
Appeals against magistrates' court decisions:			
Conviction and sentence	2,868	2,459	5,327
Sentence only	4,090	2,574	6,664

99% of successful applications to the Crown Court covered payment to a solicitor and one or two barristers.

Table 11.5

Criminal public funding: Successful public funds applications to the Crown Court, by type of proceeding and extent of public funds granted, 2005

	Solicitor Only	Solicitor & Counsel	Solicitor & two counsel	Counsel only	Total applications granted
Trial on indictment	6	2,485	2,083	8	4,582
For sentence or to be dealt with	20	4,728	7	86	4,841
Appeals against Magistrates' courts decisions					
Conviction and sentence	4	1,351	1	3	1,359
Sentences only	2	1,611	0	5	1,618

Publicly Funded Legal Services Expenditure

The Department for Constitutional Affairs provides a grant to the Legal Services Commission to cover the net cost of the publicly funded services it provides.

Table 10.6 shows net publicly funded legal services expenditure during 2005 by category of funding granted.

In 2005 total net expenditure on publicly funded legal services was £1,983 million.

Table 11.6
Publicly funded legal services expenditure 2005

	Net Payments (£000s)
Community Legal Service:	
Civil and Family Representation	524,077
Legal Help	295,827
Total	**819,904**
Criminal Defence Service:	
Higher Courts	676,614
Magistrates' Courts, Duty Solicitor, Free Standing Advice and Assistance	486,824
Total	**1,163,438**
Total Publicly Funded Legal Services	**1,983,342**

Other Publicly Funded Legal Services Statistics

Detailed statistics on the Legal Services Commission's administration of publicly funded legal services are included in the Commission's annual report for 2005/2006.

Criminal Public Finding (Indictable Offences)
Applications filed for representation in the Crown Court, 1995-2005

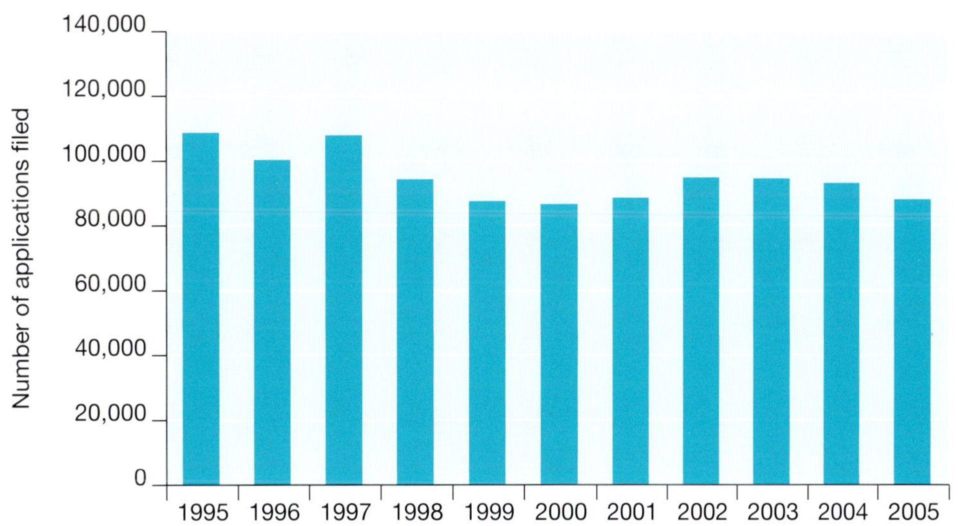

Data Quality and Sources

Please note that the data in this edition of Judicial Statistics relates to the calendar year 2005 at which time the Performance Directorate within the Court Service (an executive agency of the Department for Constitutional Affairs (DCA)) collated and published the data on behalf of the DCA. Since 1st April 2005 the Court Service has ceased to exist and the agency has merged with other elements of the DCA to form Her Majesty's Courts Service. In addition has become part of a larger Division and is now known as the Performance Directorate.

Enquiries regarding the data in this edition should be directed to:

Alan Sealy
Performance Directorate
4th Floor Steel House
11 Tothill Street
London
SW1H 9LH
Tel: 020 7210 0378
Fax: 020 7210 0382
Email: alan.sealy@hmcourts-service.gsi.gov.uk

Provided in this chapter are the sources of each data series. Where information is provided specifically for this publication the telephone numbers for the originating office are provided as readers may wish to contact the relevant office directly.

Chapter 1: Appellate Courts

All information within this chapter is provided specifically for this publication.

For individual queries regarding the data published within this chapter please contact the relevant office as given below.

Tables	Data Source	Contact Number
1 – 1.2	Privy Council Office	020 7276 0486
1.3 – 1.6	Judicial Office	020 7219 3106
1.7 – 1.8	Criminal Appeal Office	020 7947 6908
1.9 – 1.11	Civil Appeal Office	020 7947 6216
1.12	Chancery Division, RCJ	020 7947 7518
1.13 – 1.15	Administrative Office	020 7947 6908
1.16	Family Proceedings Dept, PRFD	020 7947 7305
1.17	Total of all tables	–

RCJ – Royal Courts of Justice

PRFD – Principle Registry of the Family Division (a division of the High Court).

Chapter 2: High Court – Chancery

All information within this chapter is provided specifically for this publication.

For individual queries regarding the data published within this chapter please contact the relevant office as given below.

Tables	Data Source	Contact Number
2.1	Total of all tables	–
2.2, 2.4 – 2.8	High Court	020 7210 0375
2.3	Chancery Chambers, RCJ	020 7947 6877
Patents Text	Patents Court, RCJ	0207 947 6778

Chapter 3: High Court – QBD

All information within this chapter is provided specifically for this publication.

For individual queries regarding the data published within this chapter please contact the relevant office as given below.

Tables	Data Source	Contact Number
3.1	Total of all tables	–
3.2 – 3.11, 3.15	High Court	020 7210 0375
3.12 – 3.14	Admiralty Marshall, RCJ	020 7947 6111

The Admiralty Marshal also provides Commercial Court text. High Court also provides data for the Technology & Construction Court.

Chapter 4: County Court

The majority of the information in this chapter was collected and collated electronically within the Performance Directorate of the Court Service on a monthly basis. Some information is provided on manual forms and some is on a sample basis. Details are provided below.

Tables	Data Source	Contact Number
4.1 – 4.2	Total of all tables	–
4.3	BMS & CPC	020 7210 0375
4.4	CPC	020 7210 0375
4.5 – 4.8	Stats Module	020 7210 0375
4.9 – 4.18	Small Claims & Trial Sampler	020 7210 0375
4.18	Registry of County Court Judgements	020 7391 7288
4.19	BMS & Stats Module	020 7210 0375
4.20	BMS & MBR	020 7210 0375
4.21	BMS	020 7210 0375

The ***Business Management System (BMS)*** is available in all county courts. It provides a system by which managers of all levels within the organisation can monitor and assess the workloads of all courts. Information is provided on a monthly basis 10 working days after the end of the period to which it relates.

CPC (Claim Production Centre) is the Bulk Centre situated in Northampton, which deals with claim requests from major claimants i.e. claimants who generally issue more than 1,000 claims annually. CPC customers include banks, credit and storecard issuers, mail order catalogues, utilities and solicitors specialising in debt recover. Data are sent electronically after the end of each month.

Stats Module is a manual form completed monthly by all county courts. It provides data on a number of different matters not collected by the electronic systems. This information is available 10 working days after the period to which it relates

Small claims: This is a form completed by 29 courts (from a total of **220** courts). The sampler is carried out 3 times a year (February, July & October). **The response rate is 100%.** Forms are returned 7 working days of the end of the sampler month. Information from these forms is grossed up to E&W levels.

The grossing up of sample data is done by taking the number of forms received divided by statistical module, (SM 63 – 67) that is provided by all the courts. This gives a weighted figure that is used in multiplying actual figures.

Trial samplers: This is a form completed by **219** courts. The sampler is carried out twice a year in March and September. **The response rate is 100%.** Forms are returned 15 working days after the sampler month. Information from these forms is grossed up to E&W levels. Out of the 219, some courts are NIL and apparently don't do this kind of work. Roughly 88 courts (estimate from period Mar 03 – Mar 05) have nil returns all the time. The forms usually need chasing. We can gather how many forms the courts need to send in by using SM22-23.

The grossing up of sample data is done by taking the number of forms received divided by statistical module, (SM 22 & 23) that is provided by all the courts. This gives a weighted figure that is used in multiplying actual figures.

MBR (Monthly Business Return) – This is a monthly manual return sent by the Principal Registry of the Family Division, as there is no electronic Business Management System (BMS) available.

Chapter 5: Family Matters

The majority of information in this chapter was collected and collated electronically within the Performance Directorate of the Court Service on a monthly basis. Some information is provided on manual forms and some is on a sample basis. Details are provided below.

Tables	Data Source	Contact Number
5.1 – 5.3	Children Act Private & Public Law Forms	020 7210 0374
5.4	Children Act Private Law Forms	020 7210 0374
5.5 – 5.7, 5.9	Stats Module & MBR	020 7210 0374
5.8	BMS & MBR	020 7210 0374
5.10	Principle Registry of the Family Division	020 7947 7159

Children Act Private Law Forms – Returns are made per child that means the volume counts each child separately even when more than one child is included in an application or order. The numbers include section 8 orders and other Part 11 applications, financial applications, family assistance orders, adoptions, freeing orders, Section 30 of the Human Fertilisation and Embryology Act 1990. Monthly returns are sent by County & High Courts 10 working days at the end of the calendar month. Quarterly returns are sent by Family Proceeding Courts.

Children Act Public Law – Returns are made per child that means the volume counts each child separately even when more than one child is included in an application or order and comprise care orders, supervision orders, recovery orders, emergency protection orders & transfers. Monthly returns are sent by County & High Courts 10 working days at the end of the calendar month. Quarterly returns are sent by Family Proceeding Courts.

Principle Registry of the Family Division (PRFD) a division of the High Court.

StatsMod, MBR, BMS – as per chapter 4.

Additional notes –

- Tables 5.2 and 5.3 do not include interim orders.
- Tables 5.2, 5.3 and 5.4 contain imputed data for family proceedings courts

'Data are imputed for courts who do not respond in a given period. The estimate for each period is based on the average number of applications previously returned'

Chapter 6: Crown Court

All the information in this chapter was collected and collated electronically within the Performance Directorate of the Court Service on a monthly basis

Tables	Data Source	Contact Number
6.1 – 6.20	CREST	020 7210 0378

CREST is the name of the case management system used within all Crown court centres. All information regarding the management of a case such as dates, charge details, etc. are entered onto the CREST system. The CREST system is updated daily and downloads taken monthly. Due to the nature of the system if records are changed retrospectively then these changes will be incorporated the following month.

Chapter 7:

All the information in this chapter was collected by the Performance Directorate

Tables	Data Source	Contact Number
7.1 – 7.7	Trial monitor database (manual forms)	020 7210 0378

Chapter 8: Tribunals

All information within this chapter is provided directly from the Tribunals and is provided specifically for this publication.

Any queries about the data should be directed to Noreen Razvi on 020 7566 1323 (except where alternative contact numbers are given) in the Tribunals Directorate.

Tables	Data Source	Contact Number
8.1 – 8.16	Tribunals Directorate	
8.17	Employment Appeals Tribunal	020 7273 1054

Chapter 9: Other courts & Offices of the Supreme Court

All information within this chapter is provided directly from the sources given below specifically for this publication except for the High Court Tipstaff Form, which is provided on a monthly basis.

For individual queries regarding the data published within this chapter please contact the relevant office as given below.

Tables	Data Source	Contact Number
9.1	Office of the Official Solicitor and Public Trustee	020 7911 7116
9.2	High Court Tipstaff Form	020 7210 0375
9.3 & 9.4	Public Guardianship Office	020 7664 7578
Text	Court Funds Office	020 7947 6132

Chapter 10: Judiciary

The majority of data within this chapter is provided directly from the sources given below specifically for this publication.

For individual queries regarding the data published within this chapter please contact the relevant office as given below.

Tables	Data Source	Contact Number
10.1	Judicial Appointments Form	www.dca.gov.uk/dept/depstrat.htm#part3
10.2 – 10.3	Stats 10A & Stats 10 (Crown)	020 7210 0374
10.4 – 10.5	Judicial Policy Directorate	020 7210 8390

Stats 10A and Stats 10 are forms used within both the Crown courts and the county courts. The information provided monthly are the number of days sat at each court and also the number and level of judges sitting.

Chapter 11: Publicly Funded Legal Services & taxation

The majority of information within this chapter is provided directly from the sources given below specifically for this publication.

For individual queries regarding the data published within this chapter please contact the relevant office as given below.

Tables	Data Source	Contact Number
11.1	Privy Council Office,	020 7276 0486
	Lands Tribunal,	020 7566 1323
	Judicial Office,	020 7219 3105
	Supreme Courts Cost Office,	020 7947 7312
	Principal Registry of the Family Division	020 7947 7159
11.2 - 11.5	CREST (as per chapter 6)	020 7210 0378
11.6	Publicly Funded Legal Services	020 7210 8797

MIS (Management Information Systems)

Introduction of Management Information System Data

The information contained in this publication has been produced using the Management Information System (MIS), a new data warehousing facility drawing data directly from court-based information systems. The new facility enables the Department access to more complete data than was previously possible. In some instances this has meant that previously published figures will have changed, since the new facility has also enabled the Department to include late submitted data and also to revise erroneous data included in previous publications.

Printed in the UK by The Stationery Office Limited
on behalf of the Controller of Her Majesty's Stationery Office
ID 185203 05/06 AM4298